Summer's Lease

Summer's Lease

how to cook without heat

Thom Eagle

Hardie Grant

QUADRILLE

Publishing Director Sarah Lavelle
Copy Editor Lucy Kingett
Editor Susannah Otter
Assistant Editor Stacey Cleworth
Cover Design and Illustrations Will Webb
Junior Designer Alicia House
Typesetter Jonathan Baker
Head of Production Stephen Lang
Production Controller Nikolaus Ginelli

Published in 2020 by Quadrille, an imprint
of Hardie Grant Publishing

Quadrille
52–54 Southwark Street
London SE1 1UN
quadrille.com

Cataloguing in Publication Data: a catalogue record for this book is
available from the British Library.

Text © Thomas Eagle 2020
Design © Quadrille 2020

ISBN 9781787135338

Printed in China

CONTENTS

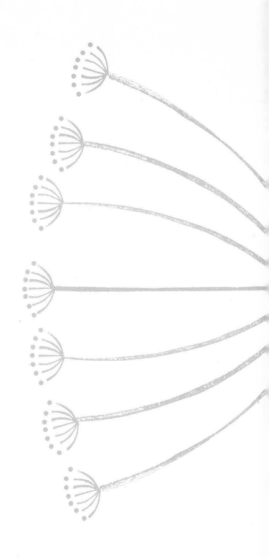

INTRODUCTION

When I think about eating, I think about bread, and when I think about bread, I think about breaking; we break it at every stage of its life. When our ancestors shared food with somebody (which is one way of falling in love) they said they were breaking bread together, and a companion is someone with whom you share that broken bread. Loaves of bread crack and sing as they come from the oven, crusts shifting as they cool on their bent wire racks, and before that, a long time before that, came the pounding and breaking of grain, to smash the seed apart before panning through it like mud in a hopeful river. We have to break if we want to eat, but luckily we love to do so. When scholars of the future come to examine the tragedy of humanity, they may well consider our fatal flaw to lie in this love and in our persistent belief that once we have broken something we can always put it back together again. That we cannot – or in other words, that some consequences are permanent – is, to my mind, the chief lesson to be gained from the Biblical story of Eden, although the subsequent arrival and sacrifice of Christ complicates the moral somewhat. Classical myths, as is often the case, provide us with clearer lessons.

Persephone, the daughter of Demeter, was picking flowers in a soft meadow in Sicily when the trouble began. As she gathered roses and crocuses and beautiful violets, irises, hyacinths and narcissi, Hades, the king of the underworld, saw her beauty and broke through the hot earth to snatch her away – and there the story might have ended. Gods do have a habit of getting their way. Demeter, however, loved her only daughter and, seeing her missing, began to search for her across the face of the earth. She looked across the fertile hills of Sicily and the silted banks of the Nile; she scoured Anatolia and the windy islands, and all across the plains of Greece, and found no sign. No one could give her any word of her daughter. Tired, eventually, and at the end of her tether, Demeter rested, seeking refuge with the Eleusinians in the guise of an elderly woman. Satisfied with the hospitality she received, she gifted the scion of Eleusis with wheat, and helped him scatter it across the earth. At this point, the story leaves the wheat behind and moves on to other things, which is a shame. It would have been good to know what exactly was made of this new grass, stronger and more fruitful than the wild blades that had been previously seen across the plains and the sweeping hills. Presumably it was first boiled whole as a kind of porridge, as Sicilians still do for the Feast of Saint Lucy, a process that requires days of soaking and hours of simmering; eventually somebody must have tried to break the grain, and found that it was good.

Demeter, meanwhile, had discovered the location of her missing daughter and persuaded Zeus to intervene on her behalf. The underworld, however, was governed by suitably inverted laws, including the law of hospitality. Whereas elsewhere to break bread at someone's table guaranteed you their protection, in Hades' kingdom it made you his prisoner. Demeter's daughter knew this, and suffered for her refusal, but had been unable to resist just six seeds of a glistening pomegranate from Hades' gloomy orchard. She had thought herself unseen, but kings and gods have spies everywhere. Technically, she should have been lost to the upper land forever, but a deal was struck, and it was agreed that Persephone would spend six months a year as the queen of the underworld – and for six months Demeter, goddess of the harvest (she of the grain) would mourn. Even fertile Sicily lies comparatively barren during this time, if you ignore the gleaming groves of orange, lemon, pomelo and indeed pomegranate that still dot the island. Summer and the seasons in general, therefore, were not, to this way of thinking, an essential part of nature or the inexorable consequence of the rhythms of the sun and of the planets, but rather the result of a series of an entirely preventable calamities caused chiefly by lust and by hunger: natural and divine history provide the model for humankind. This being the case, however, the consequences were not only accepted, but celebrated; worshippers of Demeter and Persephone in whatever form did not, to my knowledge, try to liberate the latter from her contract and let the mother reign over an eternal bounty. Persephone goes under every year without fail, and Demeter mourns, and so we have winter; but it is because we have winter that we can have summer. The meaning of summer is that it is fleeting, and so we gorge ourselves upon it, taking everything we can from the season.

The American chef Dan Barber remarks, in the short film *On Authenticity*, that he wants the cooking in his restaurants to be so seasonal that by the end of a season his chefs are sick of that period's produce. By the end of summer they should be so sick and tired of tomatoes that they cannot wait to see the end of that blushing abundance, so they look forward to the months of squashes and brassicas as they otherwise might to truffles or asparagus, and so on, throughout the year. Only by wringing the utmost from each season, or even each passing day, he seems to be saying, can we really appreciate the next. This is true enough, I suppose, but a glut of peaches does not mean that you have to sit down every day and eat peaches. A large – and for most of our history, necessary – part of summer cooking has been laying down stores for the winter; taking what can be kept of the season and saving it for the next.

I love the food of summer, but while the heat of summer lasts I do not like to cook in the conventional sense of the word. It seems pleasant, of course, to cook outdoors – to smell the smoke of wood and fat drifting across the garden or the courtyard or the beach – but the period of the process that involves standing over a hot fire in the hot sun is, in practice, not; as for cooking indoors, the less said about it the better. When I think of the things I miss from the professional kitchen, standing in an enclosed space with the dry heat of an oven on one side, a rolling steam table on the other and a deep-fat fryer in the corner, impregnating your hair with particles of grease, is not something that comes high up on the list. Everything else in the summer kitchen, though, I love. Chunks of ripe and dripping tomatoes, eaten just with salt, leaves crisp from iced water, chopped hard-boiled eggs; dishes that are more arrangements than recipes, of fish or meat or cheese or vegetables, which might be cured or pickled, sliced or whole, but are by and large uncooked: that is to say, they have not been transformed by heat – but that is not to say they are *untransformed*.

The history of cooking is a long and fascinating one, and walks hand in hand with the history of mankind. But around it dances the history of not-cooking – of all the things we do to our ingredients apart from subjecting them to intense heat which, if anything, is more fascinating; it certainly takes in a wider cast of players, including not just the cooks, but the animals and the farmers and the bacteria and the yeasts that inhabit them all, and involves a wider range of processes. Even things that are eventually to be cooked require other transformations before that final application of heat. Bread, for example, needs the hard grain broken, not just once but again and again, before being wetted and pounded again and fermented, transformed by yeast and bacteria in a way that in other contexts we would call decomposition or simply rot; you repurpose processes that seem made for destruction and use them to create. What cooks do, in other words, along with charcutiers, butchers, fishermen, picklers, cheesemakers, brewers and everyone else involved in the business of edibility, is best defined not just as cooking – by the tongs and the pans and the stove – but as metamorphosis. We change ingredients, sometimes irreversibly, sometimes for the better; or rather we change things into ingredients, and ingredients into food and food into ourselves.

The techniques of this kind of metamorphosis are ingrained in all kinds of food preparation, cooked or uncooked, but it is when they are allowed to stand by themselves, away from the crudity of

heat, that they really come into their own; it is also then that they are
most suited to the needs of summer. Summer, of course, is abundant.
Even away from the flowers of Persephone's fertile island, markets
and greengrocers and gardens are piled high with courgettes and
tomatoes, broad beans and peas in their pods, strawberries and
raspberries that give way to cherries as the season goes on – but at the
back of our minds, we know that the season will die; that it will give
way first to the rot of autumn and then to the cold of winter, and that
as it draws to a close we have to do our best to preserve of it what we
can, to lay down little bits of heat and light against the coming cold. Of
course, this was once a matter of absolute necessity; given humanity's
unfortunate inability to hibernate, the abundance of summer needed
spreading out across the colder parts of the year in order to give the
winter cook something to cook with, and the winter eater something
to eat. This borrowing from summer is now done chiefly with the can
and with the freezer (insofar as it is necessary at all, the steady march
of human progress having to a large extent annihilated the seasons),
and so older and more interesting methods of preservation have been
rendered largely useless. This, however, only means that we can enjoy
them more fully.

I hold no brief against canning and freezing, which both serve
a vital role in our modern food system, but the fact is (good tinned
fish aside) that their products to me are simply not very interesting.
They are ways of holding something in stasis, which is all well and
good, but how much better to transform! Think, for example, of a
jar of passata – tomato pulp strained and cooked and sealed. You
can use it in place of fresh tomatoes to make a ragù or a sugo in

6

the depths of winter, or in any other time or place when good fresh tomatoes are not readily available. It is a substitute, which is fine. Then think instead of good tomato purée – not the supermarket stuff in tubes that tastes of coins, but the clay-red paste of Sicily and Turkey, salty and rich and full of depth; through sun and air and time the tomatoes have been completely changed, and cannot be changed back. It is tomato concentrate, but if you mix it with water you don't get tomato juice. Cook it into a sauce and it will thicken and deepen it, adding a flavour that is not entirely that of tomato but rather all of its own; this is what you can do without cooking.

Here again, though, I am talking about an ingredient, a product that although not cooked itself is intended ultimately to be cooked – to be mixed and blended with other things and heated – whereas the finest products of transformation are proudly edible raw. Today, no one needs to make a dry-cured ham of any animal, whether in the Faroe Islands, the Iberian hills or at the foot of the Alps; after slaughtering their sheep, their black-footed pigs or their goats, they could, if they wanted, just cut them up and put the whole lot in the freezer. That they do not is testament not to need or tradition, but to pleasure. Transforming the meat in this way is often expensive and it is difficult, at least in the sense that it requires knowledge and skill, but it is worth doing because it tastes good – it is a delicacy that people across the world will buy and enjoy. This is the case with all the products of metamorphosis. Even the current vogue for fermentation, which has London in its grip and which is often discussed in terms of personal health, is really popular because of the flavours it provides, which seem as magical now as they must have done ten thousand years ago when someone's apocryphal cabbage left in a jar was found, like their meat dropped in a fire, not to be ruined but entirely transformed.

When you begin to look a little more closely at these transformations, categories begin to emerge: dishes and techniques from across different cultures and times unified by the common thread of whatever is being done to the ingredient; these may require more or less intervention on the part of the cook, and vary in their complexity. In compiling these notes I have tried to arrange them as such, taxonomizing the disparate recipes into four distinct categories: breaking, salting, souring and ageing. At least, I have kept them as distinct as I can. Each category moves forward to the next – one must break in order to salt, one must salt in order to sour, and sourness helps your ingredients to safely age. Inevitably there is some crossover between them, but in any case, they all come together in the last. These techniques are not by any stretch of the imagination new, either to humanity or, in most cases, to the average European home cook; nor do they stem from the cultish dietary theories expounded by quacks of various stripes who labour under the names of raw food, paleo, ketogenic or simply low-carb. They are rather a compendium of intensely practical measures from across times and places in which cooks have, due to the searing heat of summer, a lack of firewood or a kitchen, been unable or simply disinclined to *cook* in the conventional sense of the word but, still needing to engage with the business of dinner, have found other ways to encourage food to become edible.

Having said that, it is perhaps inevitable that practice gives birth to theory – which is certainly preferable to the other way round. The atmosphere of the professional kitchen is still, for the most part, one of controlled violence, intensely carnivorous and masculine, which the recent trend for so-called live-fire cooking has done little to change; a whole genre of cuisine and cookbooks could be summed up with the title 'Men Do Things to Meat'. Pickling, curing and even (perhaps counterintuitively) breaking our ingredients offers a different and more gentle approach, in which the focus is less on what we can do to them than on what they can do by themselves; cooking becomes less an act of interventionist force than one of nurture – of helping your meal become what it intends to be.

ON BREAKING

You can't make an omelette, as the saying goes, without breaking a few eggs; and while the omelette shares this characteristic with all ways of eating eggs – unless you intend to wear the shell away with acid or with time – the preparation of an omelette of any kind requires that they be doubly broken, once at the skin and again at the heart. There are as many recipes for omelettes as there are fish in the sea, if you include within that category tortilla, frittata and kuku; and even within the tradition of the folded French omelette instructions vary widely between a few turns of the fork and a heavy beating; but they all begin the same way – break the eggs, and beat them. It is a sad consequence of our recipe-focused cooking culture that not enough attention is paid to this fact.

Before you can cook almost anything, in fact, you have to break it first; the few things you don't will be broken in the end. If, to put it another way, you think of harvesting and preparing and cooking and eating not as separate processes but as part of a continuum, a circle from soil to soil, it is clear that the whole of cuisine tends towards destruction; the choices we make regarding food mainly concern where in the circle the majority of that destruction takes place. Wheat, for example, is edible to us as a whole grain, and was presumably mainly consumed in that form by our distant ancestors, before the invention of the millstone and the sack. It is, however, hard and close-packed, keeping its nutrition deep within itself, and so for us, as humans, to eat it – both physically to chew it and then to digest the result – whole wheatberries first need to go through a lengthy process of soaking and then boiling, the heat softening and the water hydrating the dense structure; it is the cooking, in this case, that breaks.

This is, in general, the primary purpose of cooking. It's true that often things that are cooked taste better than things that are not – as in the Maillard reactions caused when browning meat and baking bread, or the green fullness of a well-boiled head of broccoli compared with the same vegetable in its raw florets – and I don't think the effects of taste and greed on the development of cooking and therefore of civilisation should ever be ignored, but the taste is only symptomatic of the material fact that the ingredient has been broken. I believe it is now generally accepted amongst anthropologists that the discovery and subsequent development of cooking was among the most important factors in the evolution of our ancestors into something recognisable as human beings.

If you live on raw vegetable matter, as apes and some lifestyle gurus may well attest to, then you have to spend a significant amount of time – and therefore energy – chewing it. Bark and stalks and even leaves are tough in their raw condition, and need grinding down finely between the molar teeth before they can be comfortably swallowed; even then they are difficult to digest in an omnivore's single stomach, much of their goodness unavailable. Cooking, which in this case means heating through until the cell walls breach, is a way not just of sidestepping this whole procedure, but of going beyond it. Not only is your cooked head of broccoli much quicker to chew, your body can get much more out of it thanks to the, as it were, 'preliminary digestion' done in the cooking. With more of the body's work outsourced in this way, we had energy to spare for the growth of our brains, and we also had more free time in which to occupy them. It is cooking that makes us human, and that is because cooking is breaking. It is just a short step in evolutionary terms from the first roast dinner to *La Gioconda* and thence to the nitrogen bomb. Breaking, of course, is only half the story; many of our problems arise because we think we can put things back together again.

There can't be many people in the world who eat the majority of their grain in the form of wheatberry porridge. Whatever else is done to it afterwards, wheat is these days most commonly turned into flour, ground more or less finely by one of a variety of methods. I visited recently a durum wheat mill in the interior of Sicily, which grinds a blend of the local hard wheats into the two grades of semolina flour used for the soft bread and the hard pasta of the south. The process from raw grain to sack requires, after cleaning, eight separate stages – first milling and then sifting, the bran at each step put to one side for a variety of other uses. This was done entirely by machine. A network of pipes carried the grain from floor to ceiling, up above to the great shuddering machines that sifted and sorted, down below to the quick steel rollers – all was in constant motion. Even with double doors upstairs and downstairs wide open and with the ventilation fans chugging away the air was full of flour, which caught in the throat if you breathed too deeply and coated everything in the room like ancient dust, or drifting smoke.

As a child I remember once or twice stealing a few ears of wheat from the fields that start just a few minutes' walk to the south of Canterbury, close to my parents' allotment, where we would often go for walks or to pick blackberries, or, at other times, to sledge and throw snowballs. Once home, I sat in the garden and attempted, with the aid of a couple of stones, to make flour. My tools, it is true, were not the best. Millstones of whatever kind are rough – two rough but level surfaces used to sand the grain apart. I used, if I remember correctly, two quite uneven pieces of flint, which is jagged but smooth; and so I was attempting not to grind, but to forcibly hammer the grain, which was, I imagined, how our long-distant ancestors went about things. This hammer method of mine only really worked if you attempted one grain at a time, and if I ever got as much as a teaspoon of flour it is less a testament to my ingenuity or perseverance than to a purer love of hitting things with rocks.

If you have never had the chance to see inside a functioning stone-grinding windmill then you should imagine its output as somewhere between these two extremes. While not as laborious as my attempts, it is slow, as it always has been. Slow, and dangerous – flour dust is extremely flammable – and requiring the design and construction of large, single-purpose buildings which still dot the countryside of Britain and elsewhere. But it was done because it had to be – you had to break the grain apart if you wanted to eat it, and in general you had to eat it if you wanted to live. Everywhere that wheat is a staple this is understood not just in a practical but in a symbolic way. Go to Fez and you will still see discarded loaves of bread picked up from the floor, shoved in the cracks between buildings and left for the poor; like the feet of angels, bread should never touch the base earth.

To return to the point, however, breaking is essential to all forms of cookery, but it is even more so if you don't intend to do anything else to your food. As we have already seen, the purpose of preparing food is largely the outsourcing from the human body of much of the process of eating and digestion, and as we as a species have developed the practice we have evolved in tandem and have reached the point whereby there are things we can no longer do for ourselves, or at least not comfortably; we lack the teeth to do so. Luckily we have developed tools to take their place, and in some cases, a whole chain of people to do it for us. We lack the strength and the bite to take a chunk of flesh out of a recently living animal and chew it down, so we bleed it, skin it, break it into pieces and age it. Those pieces might be cooked as they are, or broken again and again, until you can eat it with a spoon, as softly as if it were cooked.

Çiğ Köfte

Much of what follows will, by the nature of the processes involved and by the lightness that summer generally requires, be perhaps more along the lines of accompaniments and snacks than meals and dishes as such. I do not wish, however, to give the impression that this heatless cooking is somehow tangential, removed from the serious business of applying fire to meat. The act of breaking in particular is fundamental, but often, as in the case of wheat, it is hidden from the eater and even from the cook. Occasionally, however, it is brought directly into the dining room and given centre stage, applied to more substantial parts of the meal. The culinary practice of physically breaking meat has by and large fallen out of fashion in this country; escalopes of veal go unhammered, the steak mallet is no longer an essential part of the chef's toolkit and the duck press exists largely as a piece of retro kitsch. In general, this speaks of a higher quality of ingredient that doesn't require such forceful tenderizing, but even the most delicate cut of steak will require a little work if you do not intend to cook it.

It took me a while to come round to the idea of eating raw meat. I remember in my first kitchen job encountering a carpaccio for the first time and being slightly baffled by it. My head chef explained that somebody had figured out that if you sliced beef thinly enough you could eat it raw, but gave no particular reason why anyone should do so; he said it as if the history of humanity had been one long attempt to eat our meat raw, the project finally coming into fruition with the beef carpaccio, when it seems clear that in fact the opposite is largely the case. As I was vegetarian at the time, I didn't think much more

16

about it. It wasn't until years later, across the course of a number of visits to France with family and friends, that I came around to the practice, although not in the form of a carpaccio but as steak tartare. I was by this point gleefully omnivorous, and delighted in trying the various and more or less edible delicacies of French meat cookery in the bistros, railway-station cafés and the like where we usually ate. I can still taste in the back of my mind the last andouillette I tried, smothered in sweet onions in a too-warm Toulouse restaurant; I often wish this was not the case. Steak tartare, however, I am always happy to think about.

It is one of the dishes most often messed around with by restaurant kitchens (my own included), and often to great effect, but even the classic version allows for a great deal of variation. You have the beef, of course; simple enough, you might think, but firstly there is the question of which cut to use (tender fillet, rich bavette) and then of how you break it. Incidentally, the name of the dish itself refers specifically to the fact that it is broken rather than to its rawness or its seasonings, which you might think were more obvious traits. The supposed origin story is that Tatar horsemen would keep a piece of tough meat under their saddles during long rides, which, when they came to a rest in their journey, would then be tender enough to eat raw. This is one of many such stories that persist in the purported history of food, and which possess the quality of being perfectly plausible until you think about it for a minute or two. Be that as it may, even a thoroughly tenderized steak is too tough for most of us to eat as it is, so we have first to do a little more by way of breaking, either by hand (or at least by knife) or by machine. I have had tartares that were essentially a pile of pre-minced burger meat, put through quite a fine grinder and served cold from the fridge, others where the meat was chopped by hand into pieces almost but not quite too large to chew, and many variations in between.

None of these is necessarily better than any other (although eating meat cold enough to hurt my teeth was an unusual experience) but what they do, when considered side by side, is show you the importance of texture as a factor in how something tastes; and the texture, of course, is a consequence of how you break it. Sometimes our tongues like a little something to work against, and the coarser texture of a larger cut provides that, giving the impression of a correspondingly larger flavour. Conversely, as you might expect, smoother-textured foods can seem smoother in taste – almost, if you're not careful, to the point of blandness. What this means in practice is that steak tartare, along with anything else that is broken quite finely, needs heavy seasoning to counteract the deadening effect of its preparation. A classic steak tartare, which might be prepared for you in the kitchen or by yourself at the table (I have more than once, in fact, been given the choice of either by my black-clad waiter), contains, alongside the minced beef: tomato ketchup, Worcestershire sauce, Tabasco, capers, sliced cornichons, finely chopped shallots, perhaps chives, Dijon mustard and sometimes anchovies. All quite assertive ingredients. The addition of an egg yolk, which coats and binds the lot in an emolliating fat, seems strange in this context, and I tend to leave it out.

Variations on this theme found across Europe and America tend to keep, if not to the exact ingredients or even to any of the same, at least to the same kind – anything that through acid, heat or otherwise produces a flavour that appears to us as having a certain sharpness in contrast to the cold smoothness of the meat. I have served a version dressed with a fermented horseradish sauce, capers, lemon and a decent amount of salt, and even that needed some watercress to help wake it up a little. It might sound as though all of these seasonings could overwhelm the meat itself, or as the often-repeated lie about curry goes, that we add them to cover the taste of bad-quality meat, but in fact they do as seasonings should and coax out a flavour that might otherwise have been lost.

If this seasoning is necessary in the classic European iteration of the steak tartare, which retains a certain amount of texture in the meat, it is even more so in the finely minced preparations that proliferate in Lebanon, Turkey, Armenia and elsewhere, and which are a much more probable ancestor to the French dish than the apocryphal horsemen and their steaks ('Tatar' being used somewhat generically for anyone of vaguely Turkic origin by Europeans of the last couple of centuries). These dishes may well have originated as a way of making palatable not 'bad' meat as such, but rather old meat – from a longer-lived and perhaps working animal, be it camel, horse or ox – the action of grinding taking the place of the long, slow cooking such meats would usually receive. As is often the case, a dish that originated in necessity is now a great delicacy, and lean, clear cuts of meat are favoured – most often lamb. The most extreme version of these preparations is not Turkic but is found rather in the cuisine of Lebanon, which prides itself on a certain refinement that may or may not be considered a legacy of the French occupation. It is certainly the most codified of the Arab cuisines, and shares the same veneration of tenderness as does classical French cooking, in which an omelette must be reminiscent more of cloud than egg, and a braise of meat carvable with a spoon. The impression one gets when regarding the parade of fillet steaks, soufflés, butter sauces and creamed vegetables that once formed the chef's repertoire is chiefly of a cuisine designed for people without the energy to chew – the evolution away from the animal having gone perhaps too far into an elevated apathy that may partially explain the French Revolution.

Lebanese cuisine does at least provide textural contrast, with the snap of radish and cucumber and shards of crisp-baked pitta sharing the mezze table with the unctuous smears of pounded chickpeas, roast aubergine, strained yoghurt and, on special occasions, the preparation of raw lamb or kid and bulgur wheat known as *kibbeh nayyeh* or raw kibbeh, 'kibbeh' being the generic term for dumplings or pastes of bulgur mixed with meat or sometimes vegetables. Paste is certainly the word for it; where even a finely minced steak tartare is given textural contrast by the pickled and raw vegetables it is dressed with, kibbeh nayyeh, although generally served with spring onions and herbs to accompany it, is presented as a homogenous mass, the meat ground to the same emulsified fineness as mortadella or a Richmond sausage. The difficult part of this operation is not the grinding as such, but rather doing so without the meat becoming oxidized and greying, and crucially without it getting too warm; while grey, raw meat is of course not attractive, grey, raw meat that has been raised to body temperature is a danger. Traditionally, this would have been done between stones, just as wheat was ground, and it can now of course be done in butchers' shops or large restaurant kitchens under refrigeration. A good food processor can easily grind meat to a fine paste but will warm it significantly while doing so; a less than perfect solution to this is to add ice cubes to the meat as it grinds, or else, as the much-missed *Lucky Peach* advise in their mortadella recipe, to tape ice packs to the bowl of the food processor. The first method waters down the meat somewhat while the second relies both on your processor mixing well from the middle to its edges and on your having a ready supply of ice packs. Given that kibbeh nayyeh has water added anyway in the form of the soaked bulgur wheat, I would incline to the former method. I should add that when I made mortadella I didn't do either – for one thing, it contained curing salts, which are quite powerfully antibacterial, and for another, it gets cooked for quite a long time shortly after blending, unlike these steak tartares.

Bulgur wheat is cracked not simply by force but by a long soaking and boiling that breaks open the wheatberries. It is then dried – traditionally in the sun – before being crushed to a specified fineness, the process yielding a product that is extremely convenient to use, like ancient instant noodles; the finer varieties can be cooked, or rather rehydrated, simply by pouring over boiling water and leaving, covered, until it is absorbed. Even the coarsest bulgur, which is cooked in Turkey into a kind of pilaf, softens in a fraction of the time taken by whole wheatberries. It is the finest type that is most widely available in this country (outside of Turkish supermarkets) and also which goes into kibbeh nayyeh, having been rehydrated and well drained, alongside finely minced onion and various spices and seasonings. Even cuisines usually spice-phobic in their meat cookery tend to turn to them when it comes to minced meat – the British sausage tends towards hotter seasoning than is usual in our pork cookery, while the mixture of the often conventionally sweet spices nutmeg, cinnamon, cloves and allspice known as *quatre épices* is a mainstay of the French charcutier. Fergus Henderson remarks in his *Nose to Tail* that ground meat often loses its flavour and needs the help of these spices to find it again, and indeed the traditional Lebanese seasoning for kibbeh and other dishes consists of these same four as well as perhaps fenugreek, ginger, black pepper, cumin, cardamom, paprika or coriander. Although the Lebanese mixture is known as 'seven spice', cooks may be less than strict on the numbers, and in any case as the components tend towards the sweet rather than the hot they act more as a boost to the sweet fattiness of the meat than as a competing faction.

I must admit that when I ate kibbeh nayyeh, prepared as part of a beautiful mezze table by a Lebanese cook of great knowledge and skill, I didn't enjoy it in the slightest. It didn't have enough salt, for one thing – when making any concoction like this of very minced meat, especially one to be eaten raw like this or cold like a terrine, I add the salt by weight rather than 'to taste', as otherwise you simply won't add enough – but the main problem was the texture. Part of me feels shamed by this. What I disliked about the texture was simply that it was too reminiscent of, well, raw processed meat – which is exactly what I was eating. I have, in the name of nose-to-tail eating and perhaps with a certain attempted machismo, gradually taught myself to like tripe, overriding my own initial objection to the offal

– that it was simply too reminiscent of stomach – with the thought that this was something I ought to like. I also allowed myself to be persuaded out of my knee-jerk aversion to duck tongues by a positive description of their varying textures. Of course kibbeh nayyeh is a delicacy and enjoyed by many, but not so far by me; I prefer my raw meat coarser, minced by hand instead of stone, and with stronger flavours to match its coarseness. I prefer, in other words, its Turkish iteration: *çiğ köfte.*

Health laws across Turkey are such that the selling of raw meat is not worth the effort, and so çiğ köfte as a fast food has largely become a vegetarian offering, the bulgur seasoned and bound with lentils, nuts or nothing more than its seasonings. Traditionally, though, or when prepared at home, it is like kibbeh nayyeh – composed of minced raw meat along with the cracked wheat and various spices. Where Lebanese cuisine is all sweetness and shade, bound with smoothly bitter tahini, Turkish food punches with heat and smoke, sumac and chilli and lemon and garlic, and this is as true of their raw and vegetarian foods as of their grilled meat, offal and fish, which perhaps most readily spring to mind when you think of the country. I had a salad once in Istanbul composed of little more than a strong white cheese – feta in appearance but with almost the flavour of blue – and purple basil, with red pepper, lemon juice and olive oil by way of dressing. It was almost comically flavourful. Many dishes are underpinned by the deep, umami savour of dried tomato paste or red pepper paste, or both – which is the case with çiğ köfte, the combination providing a similar roundness of flavour as that offered by the ketchup and Worcestershire sauce found in classic steak tartare.

It also contains – alongside various other spices and herbs – Urfa (or isot) pepper flakes, which add a fruity, smoked flavour along with a dark colour. The seasonings, in other words, are very different from those of kibbeh nayyeh, with a balance of depth and sweetness and the high bite of alliums, but so equally is the technique.

The meat, firstly, is chopped by hand with enormous knives, curved and sharp, and so it keeps a degree of shape and texture not found in crushed or machine-minced meat. It is then mixed with various spices before being not just combined, but rather kneaded together with the bulgur, onion and tomato and pepper pastes. The spices are said to 'cook' the meat in some fashion – an effect of chilli and acid on protein which I will go into more clearly later – but it is the kneading that works the magic: a gentle breaking that slightly warms and then emulsifies the fat, making a whole that is different from both the 'meat salad' effect of many tartares and the often undistinguished putty of kibbeh nayyeh, in which the textures of both meat and wheat are discernible and broken through with the bite of spring onions and herbs. Often the more expensive and tender cuts of meat are used for this, but I prefer the more flavoursome hanger; whatever you use, it should be good quality and from a proper butcher, rather than having been aged sweating in plastic. You should also, of course, use it as fresh as possible.

400g hanger steak

1 tbsp isot pepper

1 tbsp Aleppo pepper

1 tbsp sumac

20g coarse salt

1 sweet white onion

2 juicy tomatoes

400g fine bulgur wheat

1 tbsp tomato purée

2 tbsp mild red pepper paste (biber salçasi)

a handful of parsley, leaves picked and chopped

a handful of tarragon, leaves picked and chopped

a handful of mint, leaves picked and chopped

a bunch of spring onions, finely chopped

2 lemons

First prepare the steak. You will need to trim it of all sinew and connective tissue, which is easy enough to do. Your piece will most likely have a thick layer running lengthways through it; take a sharp knife and scrape down against this layer, along its length on each side, and you should end up with two long pieces of steak. Cut away any bits of translucent skin or any fat too hard for your knife to get through.

Slice the trimmed steak, first widthways into slices and then into little cubes of about a centimetre. Spread these out across your chopping board and sprinkle over the spices and salt, then use a large knife to chop over the meat a few more times until you have something halfway towards mince. Scrape the lot into a bowl, cover and put in the fridge for about an hour.

Grate the onion and tomatoes into a bowl and mix in the bulgur wheat. When the meat has chilled and the bulgur is cool, mix them together along with the tomato and pepper pastes. Mix gently at first and then begin to knead with a certain gentle force rather than the slapping abandon with which you make bread. When you feel it come together, the starch of the wheat blending with the fat of the steak to the point at which you can form it into balls, stop.

If you're not going to eat the köfte immediately then stick the mixture back into the fridge until you're ready; when you are, mix through the chopped herbs and spring onions and a good squeeze of lemon juice, then form the mixture as you like. Properly speaking, it should be shaped into little torpedoes, given pointed ridges with your knuckles and then placed in lettuce leaves to serve. Personally, I am inclined to just pile the lot onto a plate and serve the lettuce alongside – or, with a nod to the French, a pile of chips.

Smashed Cucumber and Dressed Salad

Given that cucumber is rarely cooked, it might seem like a strange ingredient to appear in this context – its green paleness hardly able to stand the gentle treatment we normally give to it, let alone the fiercer destruction of cooking or an equivalent beating – but this timid impression is misleading; the blanched and bloated fruit now found everywhere, thin-skinned and small-seeded, are merely the creation of an insipid modernity. I often used to puzzle at the instruction found in old cookbooks to peel and deseed a cucumber before using it and assumed simply that our culinary forbears (or at least the ones who wrote cookbooks) were simply more dainty than us; it wasn't until I spent some time in the United States, where seemingly an older variety prevails, that I realised the necessity. A huge variety of cucumbers prevails across the world – small and huge, long or rounded, and of all shades of yellow and green – and many of them have skins that are not just thick but tough: of that peculiar quality that some tomatoes share, wherein the skin seems entirely separate to the flesh, and of a strength that even long cooking will not break down; more like the skin of a watermelon than of a modern industrial cucumber. This toughness is generally matched with an intense greenness of flavour that does as well cooked as in a salad. Giacomo Castelvetro, writing in 1614, notes that Italians at that time liked them stewed with verjuice or gooseberries.

Castelvetro's book, *The Fruit, Herbs and Vegetables of Italy*, written while in England as a refugee from the Inquisition in an apparent attempt to get his hosts to eat more healthily (or at least more variously), takes particular delight in salads of all kinds, cooked

27

or uncooked, and it is on these that he seems chiefly concerned about educating the English. In general throughout the book, Castelvetro maintains the tone you might expect from somebody in his position – gently erudite but deferential, keen always to point out the excellence of English produce and with favourable comparisons between his native cuisine and that of his adopted home – but the Anglo-Saxon approach to salad is too much for him to bear. Having described the perfect Italian mixed salad – composed, he says, of young leaves of mint, those of tarragon, the flowers and tenderest leaves of borage, the flowers of bucks-horn plantain, newborn shoots of fennel, the leaves of rocket, sorrel and lemon balm, rosemary flowers, some sweet violets and the most tender leaves or hearts of lettuce – he turns his attention to the proper method of washing, drying and dressing the components. This, he claims, is where the cooks of Germany and other uncouth nations, including the English, fall down.

Salad leaves, Castelvetro goes on, should be placed in clean water and turned around a few times before being gently lifted out by hand, shaken thoroughly and dried with a clean linen cloth, the aim being firstly the removal of grit and dirt and secondly creating a dry enough surface for the dressing to adhere to. Many housewives and foreign cooks, he notes, have the habit of washing everything together in a too-small bucket and tipping everything out together into a colander, with the result, of course, that any dirt is simply poured back over the leaves; and then to compound this they leave their salad barely dried and sitting in its own dirty water. The final insult is done to the dish, we are told, by the English habit of simply drenching the leaves in vinegar without salt or oil (which is supposed to be added at the table) leaving an end product fit only for chicken feed. This rant largely over, Castelvetro finishes with a presumably traditional rhyme he calls the 'Sacred Law of Salads' (*insalata ben salata / poco aceto e bene oliata*: a salad, well salted / a little vinegar and well oiled), before noting that anyone who disobeys this law will never eat a good salad in their life, a fate that he fears lies in store for most of the inhabitants of this kingdom.

I find this passage admirable for its attention to every stage of the cooking process and for the seriousness with which its author approaches his subject, but chiefly for his salad dressing recipe, such as it is, which is really not possible to improve on – especially the advice he gives to salt the leaves in layers as you add them to the bowl. Although Castelvetro is of course talking about a mixed salad of leaves, herbs and flowers, you could follow his advice for most kinds of simple dressed salads, although most non-leafy vegetables will not need the same care of washing and thus drying. You could make a cucumber salad like this if you wanted – peeled, deseeded and chopped into chunks, then salted and dressed and served alongside smoked fish – but personally I find this notoriously watery vegetable requires a more robust treatment, especially the tougher sorts of cucumber, similar to the varieties made when very young into cornichons or when older into gherkins, which really need a little tenderizing in one way or another. In Hungary, in a salad that presumably would have appalled Castelvetro, they take peeled cucumbers and slice them very thinly before salting them and leaving them to drain of some of their juices, before dressing them with some of this juice and a decent amount of vinegar. This process has the effect of almost completely collapsing the flesh of the fruit into something more like a relish.

Another method, perhaps halfway between these two extremes, is to grate them, which has a more violent effect on the flesh than just chopping. A watery variety would be reduced by this and a subsequent salting into, like the Hungarian salad, almost a liquid state, but the thicker-skinned variety, which is easy enough to find during the summer at markets or in Middle Eastern and Turkish grocers, holds its shape in strands that are nonetheless ragged enough to absorb whatever you introduce them to. The important thing to note in all of these cases is the contrast with the delicacy of Castelvetro's salad preparations. When preparing leaves to be dressed as he describes, it is vital that they are not bruised or broken, and this needs to be taken into account at every stage of the process, from carefully picking or cutting the herbs and lettuces and removing any damaged outer leaves to the care with which you wash them by hand and dry them; even the weight of water can break them.

It is the crisp integrity of freshness that a mixed salad is trying to preserve, and really the word 'dressing' is appropriate for this kind – where it should cling scantily to the outside of the leaves – and no other. In general with salads you are looking not for 'dressing' in that sense but for permeation, in which potentially plain ingredients are thoroughly infused with sharpness and fat, breaking into their cells. Think of a potato salad, for example, which is best dressed twice, once with a vinaigrette while still warm and again when cold with a mayonnaise or sour-cream based concoction; the warm potatoes absorb the sharp dressing, which seasons them through to the middle and prevents the final whole – starch dressed with dairy – from becoming bland. This is an effect of heat, of course, but it is the same result we are looking for when grating a peeled and deseeded cucumber, tearing and breaking its fibres and allowing their dressing to permeate. At this point you could dress them in almost anything, but many of the most popular choices involve fermented dairy, often mint and frequently garlic, and are found wherever hot meat, black from the grill and pungent with spices, requires a cooling accompaniment: *cacik, tzatziki* or *jajeek, tarator* or *talatouri, mizeria, ovdukh* or *raita* – cross-stepping variations from the Balkans to India via the Caucasus. You could – and people no doubt do – argue for generations about the origins of such dishes. The similarity of the Turkish, Greek and Iraqi names suggests a common ancestor, which could be any one of those countries or perhaps another, spread by the Persian empire, while the difference of the others suggests a parallel evolution. Any arguments along these lines miss the point, however, which is that it exists as a dish because it is a good idea, the seeming coolness of cucumber melding via its broken flesh with the soothing qualities of yoghurt, sour cream or kefir and the refreshing menthol hit of mint, oregano or basil to create a coherent whole.

This contrast of hot, spiced meats with cool and refreshing accompaniments is accepted as common-sense culinary wisdom – and indeed seems perfectly natural to us, as perhaps it is. Once, though, such pairings would have been made not just on instinct or on the basis of taste, but as part of the holistic combination of diet and medicine known as the Galenic or humorous system, which although as science was long ago superseded, has retained a powerful hold on the way we think about food and about the workings of our bodies in our supposedly enlightened age. In any case, its emphasis on balance in our diet, whether between hot and cold, dry or wet or in any other sense, is a welcome one. A similar system, influenced by Buddhist ideals of harmony and balance as well as by medical concerns, remains in China today – at least when it comes to planning out the range of dishes to be served at a meal. *Pai huang gua,* or so-called 'smacked cucumber', is found across the country and although it is counted as a cooling food in the traditional Chinese system, its ingredients (the cucumber aside) are ones we would consider hot or sharp: quantities of vinegar and garlic, enough of the latter to make itself felt as a spice, and depending on the region, greater or lesser amounts of chilli oil and the strangely numbing Szechuan pepper.

What is remarkable in any of these versions is the way the supposedly bland or tasteless cucumber is able to make itself felt, both through such strong flavours and after the treatment it is given. 'Smacked' is not a quirk of translation, but rather exactly what you have to do to the cucumbers – along their length with either the side of a broad-bladed knife or rather more gently with a rolling pin, not so much that they burst apart and spray your kitchen with water but just so the skin buckles and cracks along with the flesh beneath while the cucumber as a whole holds its shape. The idea is not to break it into the bite-sized pieces you will afterwards cut it into, but just to bruise and damage it. The flesh should be broken enough that the dressing can completely permeate it, the depth of soy and black rice vinegar soaking into it along with the heat of chilli and garlic and the pop of Szechuan pepper, the strength of the backdrop somehow enabling the pale flavour of the cucumber to shine out more clearly. The downside to the violence of this treatment is that the resulting dish – which in strength of flavour has more in common with what in European cuisine we might consider a pickle rather than a salad – lacks the lasting qualities of a preserve; or perhaps that isn't a downside. Rather, consider that, being broken, it will change from hour to hour as the barrier between dressing and vegetable becomes thinner and thinner and the cucumber is completely saturated with its pungent sauce.

I like to make a cucumber salad or quick pickle that goes a little beyond the gentle smack to really break the gourd apart, giving it torn and jagged edges alongside the bruised flesh. I think the idea for this came from a recipe by Diana Henry, although the seasonings are mine. This version is, I suppose, much closer to what I imagined when I first read about smacked cucumber, with real violence being done to them; the seasonings, on the other hand, are much less assertive than in the Chinese versions, to account for the force of the preparation. It is important that you season it strongly enough that it can be served really fridge-cold as she suggests – a perfect salad to eat with hot meat on a hot day.

4 thick-skinned ugly cucumbers

1 tsp caster sugar

1 tbsp coarse salt

1 tbsp white wine or cider vinegar

1 tbsp colatura di alici *or fish sauce*

1 tbsp red pepper flakes

1 tsp nigella seeds, toasted

2 cloves of garlic, crushed

a handful of mint leaves, torn

Peel the cucumbers and then hit them quite hard all over with a rolling pin or (if you have one) a kitchen mallet. They should split and squirt juice everywhere. Break them apart with your hands over a bowl into jagged pieces.

In a small bowl, mix the sugar and salt with the vinegar and fish sauce to dissolve them, then mix thoroughly (with your hands) into the cucumber. Stir in the red pepper flakes, toasted nigella seeds and crushed garlic. Refrigerate until needed.

When you are ready to eat, taste the cucumbers and consider the balance of salt, sweet and sour; adjust as you think fit, then fold through the torn mint.

A Digression on Olives

Fruit juice, whether taken from the pomegranate, the orange, the apple, the pineapple or the olive, is an extreme example of a culinary breaking in which the structure of the ingredient is totally pulverized, going beyond ease of chewing to being drinkable; although you probably don't wish to drink olive oil by the glass, it is certainly possible to do so. Professional tasting of olive oil, which is necessary to determine its grade and quality and therefore its price, essentially involves knocking back shots of the stuff and seeing how they hit the back of the throat, which is a reasonably painful experience. I find olive oil in general fascinating for a number of reasons, not least of which is that it is, unlike almost any other foodstuff you might name and certainly unlike any other edible product of the Italian countryside, unquestionably better now than it ever has been. So often in the culinary world we find ourselves, as we trudge reluctantly into the future, looking backwards for a glimpse of some beautiful ideal, of things made as they used to be made, with the better ingredients and better craftsmanship of an unfallen world, only to see as we turn around that ideal recede and slump back into the darkness. It is a relief to be reminded that technological advances are not necessarily inimical to the pleasant things in life, even if in essence these advances consist of a more efficient means of destruction.

The key to making olive oil, at least in the Italian fashion, which with typical Italian confidence they have made the world standard, is that once crushed and extracted, you want to keep it from changing – to capture the juices just as they are from the half-ripe fruit before they begin to rot or ferment and to protect them from the ravages of oxygen and light. Modern industry excels at sterility, and so olive presses today are capable of a quality undreamt of by the Romans, for all their skill and knowledge of the olive harvest. This is in stark contrast to the techniques for preparing olives for eating, which firstly have remained essentially unchanged for thousands of years, modern advances prioritizing efficiency over quality, and secondly centre around changing the fruit as much as is possible from its raw state, in which to put it bluntly it is disgusting, purely disgusting, eliciting a response like that of a baby biting down on a lemon. The essential component of these techniques is time, usually with the aid of salt, but they often begin with just a little violence done to the olive to help speed the process on its way. In Turkey they make what they call 'scratched olives', a slit cut into each one to the stone before consigning it to its fate; having spent an afternoon doing this with just a few kilograms of small, green fruit I can see the virtue of doing so by machine (as they must) or indeed of crushing the olives so they sit flat and deflated around the stone, as is common across the rest of the olive-eating world. This greater destruction, as you might expect, decreases the time needed to cure the olives while at the same time altering the flavour from whole and green to oxidized and bruised; these are the bargains you make with time.

An olive is an extreme example, and there are few other foods we eat that need so much done to them in order to be edible, but every fruit benefits from a little destruction. Even the process of ripening, whether enacted by sunlight on the tree or at home with the aid of a banana and a paper bag, is really a process of breaking; a softening of the hard cells as starches turn to sweetness and the fruit sits heavy with juice. A less than perfectly ripe fruit can often be helped on its way with another form of breaking. Roasting, for example, will soften the recalcitrant flesh as well as concentrating what little sugars there are in, say, the rather disappointing apricots you so often find in Britain, but to do so to a ripe one would be an insult to the tree. This is particularly true, I think, with nectarines and especially with peaches – and in general I would say that one of the latter that does not need to be eaten over the sink is barely worth eating, or at the very least represents a wasted opportunity to do so. The sporadically fashionable grilled peach is something I find disappointing more often than not, although there is much to be said for slices of peach in a glass of cold red wine. This, though, is a product of a kind of decadence of peaches. Only when you are truly sick and tired of eating them ripe (as I said, over the sink) do you need to find other things to do with the fruit, and a British summer rarely provides you with the opportunity to do so; there is something in the peach that speaks of the cloying heat of the south.

Torn Fruit

We know that fruit is always better when it is stolen – almost irresistible, in fact, as both Persephone and Eve can well attest, although the consequences in modern times are usually far less severe. Certainly I never heard of anyone receiving anything in the way of reprimand for scrumping apples from the orchards that cover the hills near my childhood home, let alone dooming themselves or their entire species to servitude and death. It is possible, of course, that the punishment varies with the fruit. Although we are generally told in English that Eve took an apple from the Tree of Knowledge of Good and Evil, it seems more likely to have been a fig or perhaps a pomegranate, such as tempted Persephone, words for apple having been in various times and countries used as a general term for fruit – as we see in 'pineapple', in the French *pomme de terre*, in the Italian *pomodoro* and indeed in the word pomegranate. Wild or crab apples are in any case barely edible, both bitterly tannic and sour in taste and hard (sometimes painfully so) in texture, and scarcely fit the narrative of temptation as do the luscious, honeyed fig or the jewelled pomegranate. It is possible, of course, that Jahweh sensibly made his forbidden fruit as unattractive as he could and that it took all the wiles of the crooked serpent to get Eve to eat her bitter prize, but I prefer to think otherwise; something like those ruby grenades, which split open to reveal treasure within treasure, seems much closer to the mark.

Where a fig, ripe from the tree, gives itself up easily, the pleasure in eating a pomegranate is in the process of doing so – like that of slowly picking apart a crab or two over a summer table – which extends the pleasure of stealing it in the first place. It is pleasurable because it is difficult. Even cherries can be eaten like sweets so long as you spit out the stones between each one, but a pomegranate makes you work, first slicing or breaking the fruit open across its middle and then extracting the seeds, either violently, holding it cut-side down in the palm of your hand and striking the bottom with a wooden spoon or spatula, or gently, one by one with a pin, savouring each as Persephone did in the garden. Alternatively, you can gently break the pieces into a bowl of water; in theory, the pithy membrane and any stray pieces of skin and dirt will float away, leaving you with a sunken bowl of ruby seeds, but in practice this never seems quite to work, and in any case the whole process washes away a fair amount of the juice and the flavour. Best to keep to one of the first two methods, and whichever you choose, to do so carefully: a pomegranate is made of sour-sweet juice held in bitter cages, and the more you crush them the more bitterness is released; a little tannin is bracing when you buy a cup of juice from a street vendor on a baking Istanbul day, combining with the sugar and the acid to revive you like a Sicilian granita, but too much will ruin it. Break gently, in other words, with care and with purpose, as of course you should do everything.

I grew up in Kent, and so as the days got longer and the heat increased we would often go to one of the many pick-your-own farms that still dot the countryside – with a 'one for me, one for the basket' approach I still find myself adopting whenever I have to pick anything. At first, of course, I preferred the uncomplicated sweetness of the strawberry, before transferring my favour to the more tart-edged raspberry. Now, if pushed, I suppose I would defend the cherry against all comers, unless I was walking along a brambling hedgerow and eating blackberries as I went; but in the later part of the summer, when the sun is more intense, grass and grain begins to crackle and brown and your parents wait daily for news of the inevitable hosepipe ban, I find myself craving the sharper flavours of plums, their acid and tannin bracing against the heat, a reminder of colder days to come. I especially find myself craving a greengage.

Partly, I think this is just because of the fact of their greenness, surprising in a ripe fruit, which seems to carry with it some of the freshness of unripeness, with echoes of the young green plums they eat with salt or pickle or stew with lamb in Turkey, Iran and Georgia; or perhaps this is just me. Certainly I always seem to expect a greengage to be harder than it is, and sourer, though I am by no means disappointed when I bite into giving flesh that tastes sweetly of almonds. Still, there is something in the complication of the greengage that makes it work not just as an eating fruit, to be enjoyed slowly at the end of a meal, but as an ingredient within it. Giacomo Castelvetro believed that plums of all kinds should be eaten only during a meal rather than after, as was the English habit, but gives no reason why this should be the case; certainly I am happy to do either or both. Of course, you can make greengages – as with any plum or most stone fruit – into cakes, crumbles or cobblers, or stew them and serve as a fool or with ice cream or for breakfast with granola, but they do just as well, if not better, when paired with salt and lamb, pork or dairy fat, especially when the fruit is raw, and perhaps damaged just a little.

There is something very pleasing, when you begin to cook, about the cleanly beautiful lines produced by slicing fruit with a very sharp knife; the way the cut edge of a cucumber, a tomato or a plum glistens cleanly so you can see the cells have been sliced neatly through rather than smashed apart. Visual aesthetics aside, though, it is valuable when chopping an onion, a clove of garlic or a little bunch of parsley to know that you are doing so with precision, rather than bruising and hacking at their flesh; the flavour that results from the one action is quite different from that of the other. To put it another way, you will cry less when using a very sharp knife to cut an onion, which aside from the visual appeal is a good reason to use one – but sometimes it is nicer not to use a knife at all. I used to find the instruction to tear rather than slice ingredients – whether herbs, stone fruit or soft cheeses – pretentious, in the same way I find the word 'rustic' pretentious, or that sky-blue, distressed farmhouse furniture you used to see everywhere; it seemed to me to represent the kind of deliberate and feigned artlessness that can only come from a place of privilege and which, when applied to, say, lumpy mashed potato, is little short of actively insulting to the generations of home cooks who have done the best they could with scant ingredients, rather than done as little as they could to an abundance of ingredients. I still feel this in regard to deliberately lumpy mashed potato or hummus, which would rightly enrage housewives from Cyprus to Palestine, but I have come round to the idea of tearing my ingredients; it is a good way of bruising them just the right amount.

If you tear a peach, a plum or a greengage in half over a bowl, and then (having removed the stone) tear those halves again, you have not just the beginning of a dressing in the resulting juice, but also the perfect rough-fleshed edge for that dressing to adhere to, as it wouldn't to a neat slice. The same goes for pieces of mozzarella dropped in with it. Mozzarella, which unfortunately seems to be losing ground to the overrated burrata, is perfect for tearing as its structure is not granular like Cheddar or Parmesan, but rather stretched out in filaments, which tease apart easily when torn; its rich, mouth-filling blandness also matches well with tart sweetness, whether from tomatoes or from tree fruit. As for the herbs, a tear and a smack is the perfect way to release the particular scent of their oils into your nascent dressing without it being overcome by the chlorophyllic greenness that is so often the result of chopping them with even the sharpest of knives.

What follows is a series of suggestions rather than a recipe as such; the important thing is that you use whatever fruit is best – ripe enough to readily give up their juices, but not so ripe you eat them all on the way home.

> *peaches, nectarines, greengages or purple plums*
> *coarse sea salt*
> *lemon, perhaps*
> *mozzarella*
> *basil, oregano, marjoram or fennel fronds*
> *black pepper or chilli flakes*
> *good olive oil*

Tear your fruit into a bowl and toss with a good pinch of coarse salt; once the juices begin to come out, give them a little taste to see whether you think lemon juice is necessary. Peaches will definitely need some, but the others will vary from variety to variety and fruit to fruit.

Tear in some mozzarella and the herbs, remembering that marjoram and some oregano tends to be very strong, then grind over a good amount of black pepper (or chilli) and add a long slosh of olive oil. Toss all together and eat happily.

A Digression on Octopus

An Italian I used to work with who came from Abruzzo but, as
seems common, had a grandmother somewhere in the poorer south,
once told me about a summer spent with her by the sea – whether
in Puglia, Calabria or Campania I no longer recall. I was preparing
an octopus at the time; the cephalopod had arrived frozen from our
fishmonger and, now defrosted, I was removing its brain, innards
and beak in preparation for a long bath in just-simmering water with
a little white wine and bay. They would go among the rock pools,
he explained, by the beach in wherever this fishing village was, the
Mediterranean glinting forget-me-not blue into the horizon, and look
for one in which an octopus was hiding, stranded by the receding
tide (or, given that octopuses are perfectly capable of walking across
land if they have to and that, in any case, their motives are entirely
unknown to us, perhaps it wanted to be there). Whatever the reason,
when they found one, he continued, he or his grandmother would
place their hand gently into the pool and wiggle their fingers a little
in the vicinity of the octopus, at which point the curious and playful
animal would wrap one or more of its tentacles around his or his
grandmother's arm.

To be honest, I had been only half listening up until this point
– it was a blistering summer's day, I find it hard to concentrate in
the heat, and I was anyway focusing on my own octopus – so I was
therefore a little surprised to learn, as he went on to say, that with the
tentacles wrapped around him, he would plunge his hand inside the
cephalopod's head, which is open to the elements and, squeezing its
brain, whip the tentacles repeatedly against the surrounding rocks,

killing the creature as well as apparently rendering it tender enough to be sliced and eaten raw with a little salt and lemon. Now, I found myself conflicted at this point. I certainly hadn't expected my colleague's tale of childhood summers to end with him brutally beating something to death upon a rock, but I certainly don't object to death in general and I'm not sure his method is any crueller than what we usually do to marine animals, which is to let them crush and suffocate in nets or on deck. Octopuses are possessed of peculiar intelligence and sensibility, but as I was by this point braising one myself I could hardly object on that count, as much as I may have wanted to. In any case, what reservations I may have had were thrown out when I heard the words 'raw', 'salt' and 'lemon', which when applied to the population of the sea represent for me a trinity more holy than that of the soffritto, with its frankly superfluous carrot.

The idea of raw fish is, I think, generally much more appetizing than the idea of raw mammal, as the wide popularity of sushi may well show – even if in reality that sushi, purchased from a supermarket or a sandwich chain, is composed chiefly of smoked and cooked fish; it is the idea that is popular, the actuality likely falling foul of health codes and personal squeamishness. I'm not sure exactly why this should be. Perhaps it is because we associate fish (I am using this word as it once was, to cover the wide spectrum of water-born life, rather than just the vertebrates) with the cold – they are cold-blooded, live in the generally cold sea and, once dead, lie on biers of ice – or perhaps it is because of the cult of freshness that surrounds fish as the cult of ageing surrounds meat. We know – or we think we know – that the best fish is that landed this morning from a quaint little boat, and so we are more inclined to eat it raw than the well-aged ex-dairy cow the butcher had to cut the mould off. If you wander around the fish markets of Palermo or Kadıköy you will see many of the stalls crowned by a mackerel or a smallish hake, apparently twisted with rigor mortis, which on closer inspection you will see is held that way by fishing line or wire, an advertising technique which in no way lessens the fact that many of the fish on display are genuinely in that condition, still stiffened from the shock of death. You might also see buckets of cramped gurnard blowing grumpy bubbles in much the same way as the pie shops of East London were once stocked with drawers of live eels, and of course molluscs and crustaceans everywhere are sold still living, to be killed only immediately prior to, or by the process of, cooking. Personally I think this mania for freshness is misguided.

It is true, of course, that fish in general spoils quite quickly, especially shellfish which are essentially poisonous if left dead and uncooked, and the various kinds of mackerel, herring, sardine and anchovy that we group together under the term 'oily fish' – which is why these are so often around the world found preserved by salt or smoke or vinegar – but it does not necessarily follow that we should eat the rest as fresh as we do. The reason we don't eat meat in the first stages of rigor is firstly because we physically could not, as the dense muscle fibres of land animals are far too tough when tensed for our evolution-weakened jaws, and secondly because it wouldn't taste very good. We rely on the treatment of even a brief hanging to break and relax the flesh, the process of which – essentially the first stages of decay – also develops the depth of flavour, from that of a carcass to something we recognize as meat. Fish, on the other hand, living as they do surrounded and supported by water, have muscles that are, in comparison, almost unexercised – wide open in texture and even soft. You would, I think, have only a little trouble, at least where the strength of your jaw and teeth is concerned, with taking a bite out of a still-living herring – and it would mainly be the scales and skin that defeated you, rather than the muscle – and we certainly are able to eat fish immediately after death; this doesn't necessarily mean we should, though.

The idea, for example, that Japanese cuisine in general, and sushi in particular, is centred around this cult of freshness is a misguided one. The combination of fish and seasoned, slightly sour rice, now achieved with the addition of a little vinegar, originally came about through the use of the cooked rice as a fermentation and storage medium for the fish, with the acid given off by the collapsing sugar and starch more than sufficient to keep the fish from spoiling; in the process, of course, the fish was transformed into a delicacy, although the rice, having given its best, would have been discarded. Definitions and practices change, of course, and while few people still make this perhaps challenging style of sushi, even its modern iteration relies less on freshness and more on carefully controlled decay, each different type and piece of fish allowed to age and break down to its perfect point of texture and flavour; this, as I understand the matter, is as much the real art of sushi as the knife craft and the perfection of rice. In Britain, though, aside from our rich tradition of cured fish of all kinds – cold- or hot-smoked, pickled as rollmops or fermented into Worcestershire sauce – we still like our fish in the main to be as fresh as can be, although in some restaurants this is changing. Cartilaginous flatfish – turbot, skate and the like – according to conventional wisdom, are among those that need eating as fresh as possible, and it is true that if stored wrapped for more than a day or two under usual refrigeration then they will soon begin to give off a distinctive and unappetizing scent of ammonia; kept very cold, however, as fish generally needs to be, and allowed to breathe and lose moisture as ageing meat in a butcher's storeroom, and they will develop the same sort of deep flavours, all butter and umami, that you may otherwise associate with well-hung steak. Fish treated in this way in British restaurants will generally be cooked afterwards, and it is largely the improvement in flavour that is the goal, but the enzymes at work transforming raw protein and fat into these complex flavours are doing so through a process of breaking, which tenderizes the flesh as it does that of mammals, gently and silently.

Most fish, as I said, do not particularly require this tenderization if they are to be cooked, and even in most cases if they are to be eaten raw, but some, especially the apparently meatier varieties and to return to our octopus, the stranger molluscs, absolutely do. I do not understand the flesh of cephalopods; they are alien in a way that skeletoned fish are not, and their bodies seem composed of one contiguous mass, with barely any distinction between inside and out. Whatever they are made of, though, it is dense and strong and requires – as do the denser muscles of land animals – either long and slow cooking or almost none at all. Very little is enough for the smaller squid and cuttlefish we tend to eat in this country, although I once had (in a thoroughly inland village in France) a blanquette of cuttlefish with strips as thick as my thumb, and I can only assume this required further treatment, as do octopuses of most sizes (baby ones aside). Most recipes for octopus, in fact, centre as much around the process of tenderizing as they do around cooking, the former generally being very simple. Octopuses tend to be sold frozen for this reason, too; as the water in their body expands into ice it breaks the cell walls and softens the flesh rather more effectively than the traditional preface to cooking of first dipping the octopus three times into boiling water, which at least makes its tentacles curl prettily, or of adding corks to the cooking liquor, which as far as I can tell does nothing at all.

Before the invention and wide availability of freezers, of course, other techniques had to be deployed, of which smashing the creature against a rock is perhaps the crudest, if also one of the most effective. Too effective, if you aren't cautious; Aristotle, in his *History of Animals*, notes that while the octopus will soften if beaten and squeezed it has also a natural tendency to liquefy, and if overbeaten will disappear entirely. I can't say, however, that I have ever met anyone with the patience to beat one for so long. Indoors and in the absence of rocks, a similar result can be achieved by beating the octopus firmly with a blunt implement of some kind – either a meat tenderizing mallet of the sort I imagine is rarely used in kitchens these days, a rolling pin or perhaps the back of a heavy knife. Traditionally you are advised to enact this beating a hundred times in order to tenderize the animal fully, so be prepared for a workout. Even after this, an octopus would usually take a good three hours or so at a simmer to cook to softness, whether you intend to serve it boiled in a salad, stewed into a rich ragù or cooked again over a hot and blackening grill. In the Greek islands, however, and I'm sure in other times and places, they will often, if they intend to barbecue their catch, skip this precooking in favour of drying on a washing line. Cooking, of course, is an expensive practice to such island communities short of wood, while solar energy is abundant and free; a related technique is used to preserve fish in the Faroe Islands, with the bitter salt wind taking the place of the Mediterranean sun. It should be noted that even after this treatment and a good, slow grilling the result is a very different animal from an octopus that has been long-boiled. The crunch and the snap is part of the point, as it is with raw octopus.

Things to Do to Oysters

In the summer of 2018 (an unusually hot and dry summer that saw the parks and green spaces of London, at first full to bursting, eventually emptied out as the grass turned slowly browner and we finally learned why the inhabitants of hot countries so value shade), feeling the need to escape the choking heat of the city, I headed for Margate on the Kent coast where, with dog at hand, I went west instead of east from the train station. East is the town itself – the arcade, Dreamland amusement park and sandy beaches with slides, ice cream, a jellied eel stall and signs everywhere saying 'no dogs allowed' – while west, when the tide is out, is a peculiar black landscape of the sort the British coast excels in, where the land idly peters out into the sea with a slow diminuendo rather than a sudden crash. It is hard to tell whether the sea is receding from the land or the land arising from the sea; that day it seemed like a fragile network of rock held in place by the water, the rock covered here with barnacles and there with thick, slippery seaweed, the dog bounding indiscriminately between both. Usually in such landscapes you find yourself alone, but that day there were several other people there, all women wearing rubber clogs or wellington boots, some standing bent double, some crouched on their haunches and some sitting on little plastic chairs – and all apparently very interested in the rock beneath them.

The flat land and the sea have the effect of distorting distance, and by the time I had got close enough to any of the women to see that they were digging at the rock with great purpose, ignoring whole stretches before choosing their point of attack, they had already exhausted their little claim and moved on; but each left behind them a cache of what were clearly the top shells of oysters, calcium white against the dark rock. I saw now that each woman had beside her a little bucket and was shucking the molluscs straight out of the ground, leaving the bottom shell in place and dropping the flesh straight into a bucket of brine. This mining for shellfish is not something I have seen before or since, and I'm not sure why I didn't ask any of them about it. There was something so alien in the wildness of what they were doing, I think, and they were so intent in their work in that peculiar landscape that I simply felt I could not interrupt. It would have been like interrupting someone from meditation or a dream, and in any case if I had gone too close the dog would have tried to eat their oysters; I took some pictures from a distance, and carried on along the shore.

It is a shame that the sight of people digging for edible treasure should be such a rarity in Britain. We are almost all coastline, and it abounds in plants and creatures of all kinds, far beyond the few varieties we usually eat. I remember recently being struck by the fact that all the different seaweeds used in Japanese cuisine to such varied effect, some providing deep boosts of salt and umami, others their uniquely gelatinous texture, are found also in British waters; the idea of cooking with the stuff, laverbread aside, has simply never occurred to us. A similar situation prevails with shellfish. We eat crab and lobster, of course, and mussels and oysters, scallops and some of the more prestigious clams, but other species have either fallen out of favour or never been popular at all. Whelks and winkles used to be common seaside fare, and can still be found at such perhaps accidentally nostalgic establishments as the Margate jellied eel stall, but they are hardly popular; when pressed for a recipe for the former, my old fishmonger recommended I use them as bait for catching cod, and then eat that instead.

This apparent distrust of the alien is compounded in Britain by our general fear of wildness. We have, in common with mainland Europe, an abundance of different fungi in our varied woods and farmlands, from the familiar field mushroom to morels, scarlet elf cups, wood ear mushrooms, chicken of the woods, oyster mushrooms and various boletes, including the highly prized and otherwise very expensive penny bun or cep, but gathering them is something we tend to leave to the professional forager – apart, perhaps, from the occasional puffball if found pristine at the height of the season. We are scared, of course, of poisoning ourselves – as we are right to be, some varieties of fungus being very poisonous indeed – but that fear does not stop mushrooming from being a popular activity in Poland and Italy or in France, where mushroom identification is one of the duties of the country pharmacist. If I find myself in the countryside towards the end of the summer I will often go picking blackberries, but even the popularity of wild garlic and nettles in the late spring do not seem to have led to a more general appreciation of our wild plants, with London restaurants preferring to pay for ramsons from the countryside than go searching for the three-cornered leek found all over the city.

Shellfish, which live by filtering their food from water of uncertain cleanliness, are I suppose doubly under suspicion – alarming even when pristine, but also capable when not of spreading sickness and disease. Given this, it is perhaps unsurprising that the sight of people foraging for oysters and their relatives is a rare one in Britain, especially as we so often eat them raw or barely cooked. I am not among those who think that cooking the oyster is a crime against gastronomy, and although I have never tried, and possibly never will, the heavy-handed treatment of Oysters Rockefeller, I have enjoyed oysters deep-fried, poached and returned to their shell, and grilled and added to a bacon sandwich – a breakfast I particularly recommend. In *Consider the Oyster*, M.F.K. Fisher has a recipe – or rather a series of recipes – for oyster stew, which if they are as good to eat as they are to read must constitute a rare treat. Castelvetro on the other hand advises making little pies with artichokes, oysters and bone marrow, a recipe I intend to try at my earliest convenience. These dishes, as good as we may imagine them to be, are I think largely the product of winter – wet fisherman's winters, which demand a little more sustenance than raw shellfish can provide. Winter is also, of course, the traditional season for oysters.

It is one of those pieces of received culinary wisdom that everybody seems to somehow know that oysters, clams, cockles and mussels should only be eaten when there is an 'R' in the month – or in other words, throughout the winter, autumn and spring but not in the height of the summer. By and large, this is no longer the case. The traditional ban was for two reasons, both to do with the warming sea, which firstly carries with it a greater risk of disease and secondly triggers the oysters' breeding season, when eating too many of them would do disproportionate harm to the population as a whole. Now most oysters, along with many other bivalves you might buy, are commercially farmed, a practice that helps both to clean and nurture our seas and to ensure a steady and sustainable supply throughout the year, at least of the standard rock oyster. Others such as the Whitstable native are still gathered in the traditional season, although the town's oyster festival is for some reason held in July, and so it is the rocks that the restaurants and stalls up and down the high street and the harbour are selling, gathered from the shell-lined beds and broken for you while you wait.

Good red wine vinegar, a mignonette dressing, Tabasco and lemon juice are all good things of course, but all that is really necessary to consume an oyster is that it is broken; rarely in fact is breaking so entirely necessary. There can be few edible things possessed of less obvious culinary potential than the oyster in its natural state. Even the lobster, that oversized sea bug in plum-blue armour, is recognisably an animal, clicking and waving its claws and feelers at you in aggressive greeting. An oyster just sits in its rock and says nothing to anyone. If it hadn't been for the women digging for them that summer day in Margate, I don't think I would have even noticed any oysters, so sunk and camouflaged were they into their surroundings – but once I did they were everywhere, the landscape suddenly opening up like an optical illusion, and you could see for a minute how these creatures, now sold on ice with sparkling wines, were once the abundant food of the coastal poor, who in a short walk along the beach could dig out enough to fill a juicy pie.

Reservations about pollution and spawning in the wild population still stand, and I would not necessarily recommend that everybody take to the seaside to gather their own, but I certainly think, if you enjoy oysters, that it is worth learning how to break them open for yourself, so you can buy a few from the fishmonger and eat them slowly on a leisurely afternoon: a small luxury that is in fact not all that expensive. If nothing else, so many of the stalls you see at food festivals and the like selling shucked oysters by the half dozen break them open quite badly, leaving the muscle still attached at the bottom and with bits of broken shell clinging to it; if you learn how simple the procedure is for yourself you will realize that you don't have to settle for such overpriced incompetence. Buying commercially farmed and landed oysters means you don't even have to prise them out of slippery rock, which I think is probably the most difficult part of the process. Luckily our more intelligent ancestors, in discovering the culinary potential of this apparent piece of striated stone, also discovered the trick for getting them open.

You could, if you liked, follow the example of the sea otter and, selecting a favourite rock, use it as a hammer to crack open the oyster against the anvil of the beach, but I think this would become quite tiring before even a half dozen had been got through, and would in any case result in quite a gritty mess you might find difficult to swallow. Far better to take your oyster knife if you have one, or a large, flat-headed screwdriver if not, in your dominant hand and hold the oyster in the other, nestling it in a tea towel to protect yourself against stabbing (you can get chain-mail gloves for this purpose, but I have always found this to be an investment too far). Insert the tip of your implement in the gap by the oyster's hinge, and when it is comfortably in, turn your hand sharply by ninety degrees, at which point the bivalve should crack open like a book. Scrape your knife along the top shell to detach the muscle, and then scoop along the bottom to detach it there as well. Check for any stray bits of shell or other grit; you can give the oyster a little rinse at this point if you are really worried about such things, but you will wash away a lot of flavour with the dirt. Either way, what you have in your hand is an oyster broken clean of its shell, and the only question now is to decide what to do to it.

The almost astringent flavour of lovage goes particularly well with seafood, especially with the slightly richer, creamier flavour of oysters gathered in the summer months. You could chop or mince it into a green sauce, or add it to the diced shallot in the traditional mignonette dressing for raw oysters. It would also go well in an oyster soup or stew, but I like just to infuse the herb in vinegar and let people dress their shellfish as they prefer. If you can't find lovage, then about twice as much leafy celery might make a good substitute. This makes far more vinegar than you will need for your oysters, but it keeps indefinitely and is also excellent in salads and sauces.

bunch of lovage (about 50g)
500ml apple cider or good white wine vinegar
6 oysters

Put the lovage and the vinegar in a jar, seal the jar and leave somewhere dark for a month before straining and bottling. (Vinegar being vinegar, there is no particular need to sterilize your glass, but it should, of course, be clean.) When you have shucked your oysters, add the vinegar to the condiment tray with your lemon wedges, hot sauce and whatever else you fancy.

ON SALTING

Salt is perhaps the one constant across the varied times and places of our shared culinary history; there is no one who eats without it in one form or another. Cooks who are sparing with the actual white granules, refined from sea or rock, might season instead with salty concoctions of fermented or cured pulses, meat and fish, and even in the absence of these, every creature we eat has salt in its veins, and you would have to walk a long way inland to find a vegetable free from salt borne in the air from the wide sea. We have to eat salt, in other words, and so we may as well learn to use it properly. Ask any chef about their culinary secrets and they will tell you, if they are being honest, that they really begin and end with salting – with proper seasoning that can draw out and maximize the flavour inherent in anything. But the uses of salt go beyond taste. It is perhaps even more vital for its physical properties – for the transformations it can enact on our ingredients. The results of these are many and varied – some quick, some imperceptibly slow, some wrought on vegetables, some on fish and some on flowers – but essentially they all boil down to one thing: salt draws out moisture.

This is, of course, very useful to the cook, since so much of cooking is really the process of controlling and moving around water. It became so standard for a while for recipes to mention salt only at the very end, when a pinch might be added to correct the seasoning, that it can be surprising and even mystifying to read one that keeps mentioning it, with salt apparently being added at every single step – but that is often how you can tell a good one from a bad one. If you want to cook onions down to a collapsing sweetness, for example, then just as important as the amount of fat you use and the heat you keep them on is the good pinch of salt you add to the pan, encouraging the onions to sweat their juice out and preventing them from burning. Those who obsess over the details of grilling meat over embers argue endlessly over the best time to add salt – half an hour in advance, just before cooking or afterwards while it rests. I can't say I have ever done much research into the matter, but I know that the crux of the argument is over which method loses the least liquid to the fire, the goal of course being juicy meat inside a good salty crust.

Of course, cooking gives you other ways of moving moisture around, too; those onions would, left unsalted, eventually collapse and give up their liquid anyway, though they might do so rather more unevenly and maybe burn a little in the process, while the debate over grilling steak shows that in the end it is perhaps the cooking that is more important. If you remove the heat from the equation, however, the salt becomes much more vital; you have to use it with a little more awareness, at particular times and in particular quantities, in order to get the results you desire. Traditional European charcuterie, for example, although in its final form really the product of time and of air, relies entirely on salt in its early stages to begin the process of drying – and most importantly to do so safely, salt being powerfully and usefully antibacterial. Too much salt or too much time and your collar of pork might turn out inedible, both in texture and in taste, but not enough and you risk losing it to rot and mould. A certain amount of the latter, of course, is desirable in some charcuterie, but it needs to be kept under control; rampant blue fur is, at least in most of Europe, considered a failing. The protective qualities of salt against this and other invaders should not be underestimated.

At the risk of oversimplifying a complex and potentially dangerous issue, if you put enough salt in something it simply cannot go off; although in this state it may not be especially pleasant to eat, you know at least that it will not harm you. Think of those cricket bats of dried fish you see in the markets of Venice and Hackney, hanging from the tops of the stalls or sitting, fanned in buckets – pieces of essentially unperishable protein that could sit in your pantry for years, accessible year-round although the seas are too stormy to fish, the weather bad for the harvest or the wolf at the gates of the city. Salt is security.

It is incredible really that such a powerful factor in the continued and widespread survival of humanity has become so demonized by certain sectors of the supposed 'healthy eating' lobby, who will tell you that salt is bad for your heart; I'm told that this is only true for those unfortunates whose rare condition makes them susceptible to it. It is not the case that salt is absolutely bad for your heart, which the rest of us should be thankful for. Be that as it may, I am aware that many people for whatever reasons wish to reduce the salt in their diet, which is fine. I am not here to tell people how to eat. There are many places where salt can be reduced, and of course the palate can be weaned away gradually from saltiness; you may find after a while that you don't need anchovies and capers and olives on your pizza, although you may miss them. When salt is used as a seasoning you can do as you like. When salt is used as an agent, however, you need to be a lot more careful. Salt, for example, is essential for bread making, acting gently in opposition to the yeast of whatever kind to prevent it from getting out of control. I have had people complain to me of their bread-making failures, explaining that they followed the recipe exactly but that, actually, they missed out the salt, as they don't like salty bread. A wonky and overrisen loaf, although disappointing, is no real disaster of course, but much more caution needs to be used in recipes involving salt and raw meat.

Salt kills bacteria, but it is not all-powerful. You need to use enough of it to stand a fighting chance against them, but generally only just enough. If you are making bacalao or wrinkly black olives, say, in the traditional manner, then you can use as much as you like, knowing that they will be in any case washed or soaked before use; with something like a cured sausage, which uses the salt as both agent and ingredient, you have to be a little more precise. A filling made with half-and-half salt and meat would be practically indestructible and certainly safe from microbial infestation, but it would also be completely inedible; luckily, much lower levels of salt do the job. When making fermented or dry-cured charcuterie, or any preparation of raw meat that is going to sit at ambient temperatures for days or weeks, you calculate the amount of salt required as a percentage by weight of the other ingredients once prepared. So in making a salami, for example, you mince your meat and your fat, add wine and spices, and then weigh this mixture. Salami, which relies on a degree of bacterial fermentation, cures best at levels as low as two to three per cent salt, so if your filling is a kilogram you would use between twenty and thirty grams of salt, depending really on taste; you would use a little more for charcuterie that is straightforwardly cured. There is an ongoing argument in the world of meat curing on the use of nitrates and nitrites, but it is not one I intend to get into here. In any case, these are questions that arise when talking not just about salted meat but about aged, dried and fermented meat and therefore belong in quite another chapter.

It is, I suppose, unlikely that air-cured charcuterie will ever become a major part of the British domestic culinary repertoire. Our climate is better for it than you might think, and it needs little in the way of equipment or even space, but making prosciutto or *coppa* is still very much a project, and if you don't have direct access to whole animals or large cuts of meat it can be a very expensive one. There are luckily much quicker and simpler forms you can make at home that, while not the full-blooded ham, rely as much on the transformative quality of salt and on the removal of water. Charcuterie of any kind is an extreme example of this, with the intention being to remove the majority of the water from the meat and discard the pinkish, salty runoff, but the same principles apply on a smaller scale to fruit and vegetables as much as they do to meat, in which case the drawn-out juices will often form part of the dish – much as the resting juices of a nicely cooked steak can, and probably should, form a part of whatever sauce or dressing or gravy you are making to accompany it. In the salad of fruit and cheese described earlier, I recommended that the greengages or nectarines be ripe enough to spill their juice easily into the bowl, but if they hadn't been then a little salt would have been the answer, rubbed straight into the cut flesh of the fruit until the moisture pools and beads on the surface and it takes on the kind of flush you would usually associate with cooking. Salads made like this often need very little else in the way of dressing, the gentler acidity of the juices not demanding a placatory oil in the way that vinegar and lemon do. You may still wish to add all of these anyway, of course, to provide a little blinking acidity to counteract the summer heat.

A note, finally, on types of salt, since the recipes that follow will be using it prominently. I am fascinated by it, historically as well as culinarily; by the lengths to which civilizations have had to go to get hold of this chemical, both inimical and vital to life. I recently spent three months in Sicily, and the day I consider best spent was that at the salt pans in Trapani, where Archimedean screws and five-sailed windpumps of Dutch design shift the evaporating water in ever-greater concentrations of salt; as it gets stronger it is populated by violently pink, salt-loving algae, which thrive with no competition in the deadly water, and which ultimately give colour to the feathers of the local flamingos. Between the pools are paths lined with sea purslane and a rare and curious fungus, and everywhere were great piles of the finished product, a coarse and dirty white, in such quantities that it was hard at first to imagine what it was – when do you ever see salt in piles taller than your head? The salt in the end is excellent, and I was glad to buy some from the car boot of one of the salt pan owners. In general, however, I find the extremes of snobbery around salt to be more than a little ridiculous. Pink salt supposedly from the Himalayas, black salt from Hawaii, grey salt from Brittany – all so often sold at high prices on the basis of their so-called purity, when in fact their differing colours and particular qualities, such as they are, stem rather from impurities; from all the other substances they contain apart from salt. Essentially, they are badly refined, and in any case I don't believe anybody should be proud of shipping a common mineral halfway around the world.

That being said, different textures of salt are certainly suited to different purposes. Professionally, I have tended to use three types: a fine salt, a coarse sea salt and a coarse rock salt, of the kind intended for grinders. Although the large and solid crystals of the latter do arguably make it marginally better than coarse sea salt for such purposes as preserving lemons, salting fish and the like, it is more due to its low price that I use it for these purposes, an important consideration if doing things on a restaurant scale. I never bother buying it at home. Fine salt, even if you buy additive-free, pure sea salt, is generally the cheapest, and of course it dissolves easily and evenly throughout whatever you are seasoning with it. Scrambled eggs in particular are more effectively seasoned with fine salt. Certainly the most useful, however, is the coarse sea salt, of the kind that can be easily crushed between your fingertips. It is good for finishing dishes and to add a little burst of texture to a plate of, say, raw sliced meat; its abrasiveness makes it especially useful for macerating the juice out of stubborn fruit; and the size of its crystals makes it much better for curing fish and flesh. Fine salt turns quickly into brine as it draws the moisture out of the meat, which tends to make whatever you are curing too salty and often dries out the surface before the centre has a chance to cure. I am aware that coarse sea salt is rather more expensive than the alternatives, but given its benefits it is that which the following recipes are written for; you can of course use whatever salt you like, but be aware that timings and quantities will differ greatly. I would encourage you, in any case, to think of salt not just as an addendum, but as an important ingredient, and to try to use the best you can afford.

A Tomato Salad

At the risk of sounding like the stereotype of a certain kind of British cook, drunk on the Mediterranean sun and venerating its produce and dishes far above their own, I think it is reasonable to say that I did not fully grasp the point of a tomato until I first tried one in Greece at the age of eighteen. Although the general quality of the tomatoes available in Britain has improved immeasurably in the last ten years or so, the so-called 'salad tomato', intensively grown year-round under plastic in Holland and taken hard and unripe from the vine to keep it easily sliceable with blunt British knives, is still common enough – if found less now in salad garnishes, where it is often replaced with cherry varieties, than in the terrible sandwiches of railway station cafés. In fairness to the British, the use of these tomatoes is by no means confined to our country; even in Sicily, where in the scorched heat of the summer they grow what must be some of the best tomatoes in the world and where, we fondly imagine, their diets are deeply in tune with the changing seasons, I have eaten salads of fridge-cold wedged tomato in February. We long to stretch out the summer. The fashionable London food world, obsessed with the language of seasonality, has embraced the longer growing seasons of both the summer and winter tomato varieties to the extent that there is now no gap between them and tomatoes are once again acceptable to eat year-round.

People can eat what they like, of course, but it seems to me that if you genuinely wish to eat a product only when it is at its best then this will sometimes involve self-denial. These days, we tend to think of seasonal eating in terms of abundance and gluts and the cornucopia of the warm south, and cast around for ways to use all these courgettes, all this wild garlic, all these blackberries; it is difficult to remember that once seasonality would have been felt like a prison. Gluts had to be used – dried or pickled or preserved in whatever way – or there might not be enough food for the winter. Produce like tomatoes would mainly have been eaten in these forms, as sun-dried tomatoes or tomato purée or fermented pastes or more recently, with the adoption of home-canning techniques, as passata, bottled whole tomatoes, and so on. We cannot now in our affluent society replicate this feeling; hunger now is a political issue, one of unfairness and distribution, not simply of there being not enough food, which is available to those who can afford it in almost nauseating abundance. In general preservation, whether of meat or fish or fruits, is done because it always has been done, and because its products are useful and good. The alchemy of tomato purée does something that fresh tomatoes cannot.

Given this, it is understandable that we are reluctant to deny ourselves things – we simply aren't used to doing so; but it seems to me that in demanding a constant supply of ingredients that once would have been a fleeting yearly treat, we become inured to mediocrity. Look at the strawberry, the British growing season of which seems to have doubled in length in my lifetime and which is in any case available throughout the year from other sources. I remember sitting in the straw with a basket of fruit that almost collapsed at the touch, sweet and herbal juice running down my chin, and I think I knew better then than I do now what a good one tasted like; it is so difficult to find one amongst all the dross, and no one seems to welcome the real strawberry season with open arms. Although to my mind somewhat overrated, asparagus has survived rather better, appreciated as a real and rare seasonal treat and apparently eaten daily by its enthusiasts – but even this has begun to suffer from our mania for constant availability. Everyone with an interest in such things knows not to buy the Peruvian stuff sold in supermarkets throughout the year, but now, as with strawberries, the British growing season has been extended, with the first crop grown indoors and lacking the real flavour. We decline into mediocrity.

Aside from the more ready availability of good imported tomatoes from Spain, southern Italy and elsewhere, the quality grown in this country has improved immeasurably. There were always people cultivating them in their greenhouses and allotments, I suppose, that without the need for longevity and resilience could be eaten much riper and fresher than industrially grown tomatoes. At the café and plant nurseries where I used to work in Suffolk, the owner was somewhat obsessed with tomatoes and the gardeners there grew, I think I can say without exaggeration, over a hundred different varieties: some more ornamental, some more delicious, small and blueberry-dark, huge and yellow, zebra-striped, virtually black, a rich green or an apricot orange or a vivid scarlet when fully ripe, a mixture of heritage varieties and modern breeds from the United States and from Europe, some suited to cooking, some to salads and some simply to eating straight from the vine. I remember especially the huge yellow one, though the name of the variety now escapes me, pulsingly ripe, with dense flesh and dripping juice, which in colour and flavour resembled mango more than anything else. These were grown in pots under plastic in an environment that, at the height of the summer, reached at least forty degrees and required, I seem to recall, an astonishing amount of work – although luckily I did not have to do it. On a more feasible commercial scale are the Isle of Wight tomatoes, which take advantage of lengthier days and the sea air to produce something that is close enough to a really good tomato to leave you wanting just a little bit more; perhaps nothing will ever live up to the imagined perfection of your first fruit.

In any case, this tomato, eaten in Athens in the summer the year I turned eighteen (although I don't remember the exact tomato as such, but rather a composite of all the tomatoes I ate there), would have been the first of the fruit I had eaten genuinely at its best, allowed to ripen fully in extreme heat, perhaps under-watered to stress the plant into a sweet brightness as they do in Sicily, but certainly bursting with flavour beneath the thick skin. I remember a deeply furrowed beef tomato eaten in wedges like an orange, though whether that was the first I tried or the twentieth I could not say. When looking for a salad tomato in the heat of a Mediterranean summer, in fact, the difficulty lies more in finding one that is not too ripe than in the opposite. In late August, when everybody picks and processes their crop, puréeing the softer ones for passata and tomato paste and halving the more shapely examples to be left in the sun and kept either dry or under oil, the time for tomato salads has already passed; it is earlier in the season, when, while still sweet and deeply flavoured, the fruits still possess a little crunch that I now think is best for them. This is the result of age and exposure, however, and at the time I was happy to eat the suddenly exciting tomato as often as I could. Vegetarian and without a great deal of money, during the month I spent in Greece I ate, besides an endless procession of cheese pies – some with spinach, some without, some heavy with dill and some brightened with mint, the pastry varying from crackling filo to something like puff which may have been made with yoghurt – an equally mutable series of tomato salads, sometimes with feta and olives and usually with cucumber and onion. Whenever I made these rather than buying them I amused myself by seeing how many different ways the few ingredients – which besides those mentioned included only salt, wine vinegar, oil and sometimes pepper – could be combined, which vegetable and which seasoning went first into the bowl and what this did to the end result.

After who knows how many repetitions of this somewhat haphazard experiment, which continued after I returned to Britain and during which I suppose I learned a lot about the action of salt and vinegar on onion and tomatoes, I settled more or less on the formula I still use now, which I remember reading afterwards is also the (or at least a) traditional Greek technique. Although good tomatoes are important, the salt is the key. The uses of salt in the kitchen are endless, but they can essentially be divided into two categories: salt as an ingredient and salt as an agent. At one end of the scale are the small amounts of it we use to enhance the flavour of everything else. Our taste buds don't really work without salt, and it is important to remember the necessity of pleasure in the face of those who would deny themselves salt, fat or any other ingredient in the name of supposed health. At the other end you have the huge amounts of salt required to make, for example, prosciutto, which sees raw pork essentially buried in salt for a week or more as the preliminary stage of a longer drying, drawing out a lot of the moisture from the meat and keeping it comparatively safe from bacteria. When the salt has served its purpose, it is discarded. Most culinary uses of salt, of course, fall somewhere between these two extremes.

In the case of this tomato salad, for example, the technique I hit upon was first to chop the tomatoes into whatever sort of pieces seemed appropriate – halved straight across for cherry tomatoes, halved on the diagonal for baby plum tomatoes and cut into irregular eighths for larger sorts – and then to put them into the mixing bowl with a decent three-fingered pinch of salt, which I would toss through the pieces of fruit, rubbing it a little into their cut flesh, before leaving the result to sit while I prepared the other ingredients. In the absence of excellent tomatoes, sweetened in the Greek or Campanian summer, I might also add a pinch of sugar to the bowl. This initial maceration, as well as being an effective method of getting your seasoning in early – salads in general requiring, as Castelvetro noted, a surprising amount of salt, which can be difficult to add in sufficient quantities at the end – also begins the process of making your salad dressing. By the time you've peeled and sliced your onions, peeled and deseeded and chopped your cucumber, stoned and halved your olives and spent some time deliberating over whether you should keep the feta in one slab to put on top of the salad, as they tend to do in Greece, or dice or crumble it throughout, which is nicer really to eat, the tomatoes should be sitting in a good puddle of their own juices, drawn out of them by the salt and the sugar. Depending on your tolerance for acidity, you might find that this juice can entirely take the place of vinegar in the dressing; I usually add some anyway, and often wish I hadn't.

A similar process is used in making the kind of fruit salad which in Italy and elsewhere is called 'Macedonia', apparently in an unlikely reference to the ethnically diverse empire of Alexander, wherein diced fruit – in winter perhaps just citrus and apples but in summer any combination of melons, cherries, peaches, apricots and later grapes, pears and plums – are macerated with sugar and a little lemon juice. The latter is really just for seasoning, as the sugar works as the salt does with tomatoes to draw the copious juices out of the fruit, forming, without cooking, a light syrup, tasting intensely of the fruits themselves, which dresses the dish. Although recipes tell you to let the salad sit for maybe half an hour before serving, it is really one of those cases where the leftovers are better – left in the fridge overnight until the fruits, by now pale and a little wrinkled, are entirely submerged in their heady juice and cold enough to be slightly painful when bitten into. The perfect breakfast on a too-hot day. As tomatoes in general dislike refrigeration, and as in this kind of preparation the goal is not homogeneity but a certain neat distinction between the ingredients, the same is not quite true of our salad; it is best once the juices have begun to pool to finish making it, and to eat. The question of exactly how to finish it is a whole other discussion, of course. Once you have your macerated tomatoes you can take them in almost any direction you like. Having eaten enough of the classic 'Greek' salad in those months of experimentation to last me a lifetime, this version is my current favourite, with the yoghurt adding another layer of acidity and turning a sunset pink as the tomato juice bleeds out into it.

8 ripe tomatoes, cut roughly into eighths
coarse sea salt
1 small cucumber, cut into chunks the same size as the tomato
a bunch of radishes, sliced
1 red onion, sliced into very thin rings
100ml thick yoghurt
olive oil
a handful of Greek basil, oregano or dill
black pepper

Put the tomatoes in a mixing bowl with a good pinch of salt – closer to a tablespoon than a teaspoon – and mix them well, rubbing the salt into their flesh and crushing them a little in your hands. Leave to stand while you prepare everything else, or for at least fifteen minutes.

Toss in the cucumber, radishes and onion, then add the yoghurt, mixing it in well so it combines with the tomato juice. Fold through a glug of oil, the herbs and a good grinding of pepper. Serve with all the dressing and some more olive oil drizzled on top.

Kebab-shop Onions

Salt is very effective when used gently, left to its own devices to perform the work of osmosis and seasoning; that it can do so quietly in the dark of a refrigerator or cellar is one of its chief virtues. If you have time on your side, then often nothing more needs to be done. Sometimes you don't, however; sometimes you want not to draw an ingredient gently out of itself but to crush it violently inwards, a process greatly speeded and facilitated by salt. This is where coarser-crystalled varieties come into their own. If you want, for example, to make a smooth paste of garlic to stir into dressings or sauces or emulsions of herbs, yoghurt, oil and so on that receive no cooking, one way to do it is to first chop a clove fairly finely, and then, spreading it out on your chopping board, to sprinkle over a little coarse sea salt. As you drag the flat of your knife across the salted garlic, you are doing three things to it. First, you are simply crushing it with the weight of your hands and of the blade; second, the salt, drawing juice from the garlic, is helping to lubricate the paste you are making; and last, both of these are aided by the abrasive texture of the salt, acting like sandpaper or the little spikes on a tenderizing mallet. That a simpler way of producing this paste is simply to grate a clove or two on a Microplane by no means lessens this excellent demonstration of the properties of salt.

This combination of salt and violence also comes together to great effect in any of the sauces traditionally made in a mortar, in which the blunt force of the pestle is aided immeasurably by the silent work of salt. I always thought these more trouble than they were worth, an archaic affectation rendered obsolete by the invention of the food processor – until I finally got a good one. I used to have a little set in green soapstone which, while palely beautiful, was incapable of crushing anything stronger than toasted coriander seeds; I have seen ceramic mortars with hollow pestles, which are just ridiculous. The most important factor apart from size – which rather determines what you can do with it, those large enough to make a batch of aioli in, as is traditionally done in Provence, being few and far between – is the weight. The burden of the work of crushing should not be taken by your arm – if it was, you might as well be smashing your garlic and herbs against the kitchen counter – but rather largely by gravity, ably assisted by the strength of the stone, and by salt. I now have a set made of black marble and I use it a lot, both for spices and for pastes and sauces, having realized that the results are very different from that of a food processor.

This is, I suppose, hardly surprising when you consider that the action of a food processor is itself completely different from that of a pestle and mortar, the former finely chopping where the latter crushes, and if the results for mayonnaise and its derivatives are remarkably similar (although a food processor produces a notably stiffer sauce) then those for pesto and other herb sauces are not. For example, the Italian salsa verde, a herb sauce heavy on parsley, is really one name for two completely different sauces, one chopped by hand and one made in a mortar, the textural pleasures of the former better suited to cold meat and the latter to stirring into a little brodo or braise, with the food-processed version being a strange approximation of both. Both pesto Genovese – what we usually just call pesto, of basil and pine nuts – and smooth salsa verde should be essentially pulverised rather than chopped, the leaves of the herbs completely broken down with the aid of salt and garlic into a smooth homogenous paste, all one green with the individual components undiscernible. The clue, of course, is in the name: a pesto is a paste you make with a pestle. You can tell the difference as you make it. I was once press-ganged into making pesto by hand for a cooking demonstration in a marquee on a rainy bank holiday weekend, the blender having decided at the last minute not to work; the aroma that filled the tent as I sweated and pounded, all pepper and menthol and sunnier places, was quite astonishing.

Force and salt, then, are a powerful combination, but they don't always have to be wielded with such weight behind them; the aim is not always to crush. They can instead be employed together as a way, in part, of mimicking the process of cooking, of softening both in flavour and texture otherwise aggressive ingredients. Take, for example, the onion, whether red or brown-skinned or large and white. So much of the flavour of a dish lies in how exactly you cook it, or to put it another way, in how you break it apart. The result of thinly slicing onions into half-moons and then cooking them very gently in olive oil, covered with a cartouche of baking parchment, is very different from roughly chopping them and cooking, uncovered, over a high heat so the edges catch; and both are different from dicing as finely as you can and sweating in good butter. In all cases, though, the idea is for the action of heat, aided generally by a pinch of salt, to break the ringed structure of the onion, and to caramelize to a greater or lesser extent the resulting juices, softening the effect of their acidity. Rarely do we put raw onions into a stew or braise, however long it is going to cook for afterwards. There is an understanding that the onion needs to be tamed.

When I was younger I would happily eat raw onion in what seem to me now outrageous quantities, with all those tomato salads heavy with thickly sliced red onion – supposedly, but not in my experience, notably milder than the usual English brown – and while I still enjoy the occasional spicy hit of raw spring onion in a salad, or even of a red, albeit in much thinner slices, I am no longer quite so willing to endure the resulting heartburn and social ostracization that invariably follows overconsumption of raw allium. If I want raw onion in my salads now, I find I have to do a little more work. Very often this is just a matter of finding the right onion. Knowing your onions, as the saying goes, is extremely important for the cook, where different varieties will behave very differently in the pan or under the grill, their levels of acidity, water and sugar determining whether they will sweat or brown, catch or char, and this is if anything more important with the subtler transformations of salt and pressure. To put it another way, as you're going to change it less, it needs to be right in the first place.

There is a notable difference between home and professional kitchens in the type of onions used, which is partly just a matter of convenience and volume – the standard cooking onion for most of my career has been the Spanish onion, at least twice the size of the usual sort available here, making a huge difference in terms of both the time spent peeling and trimming and in the resulting volume of waste. Spanish onions also tend to be somewhat milder, which, among other things, makes for happier chopping. For salads, on the other hand, rather than the overused red onion (which as I said is not particularly more edible raw than any other type), I generally use the white-skinned variety, which resemble vastly oversized versions of the silverskins sold for pickling and are most readily found in Italian and Turkish grocers. Given the choice, in fact, I like to use these for cooking as well, but that's another story. These are sweet and white-fleshed and bring barely a tear to the eye; I once saw the artist Gilbert Prousch order a whole one in an East London Turkish mangal (or barbecue) restaurant which, after eating in wedges like an apple, he declared good, if perhaps a little strong. I would not usually go that far in my onion consumption, but if you are looking for an onion to be thinly sliced on a mandoline and tossed through a different kind of tomato salad, dense with herbs, then this is the kind to go for, and it works equally well when somewhere between cooked and raw.

It is funny, really, that Prousch decided to take his Turkish onion so pale and unadorned, as the things that mangals, and Turkish restaurants in general, do with onions are really remarkable – very far from the chunks of onion, shrivelled, burnt and undercooked, which adorn vegetable kebabs at ten thousand dreary English barbecues. That restaurant in particular, in fact – Mangal II on Stoke Newington Road – does the best version of ızgara soğan I have had outside of Turkey. It is a salad of those white onions, thoroughly charred over open fire and doused hot in a dressing of pomegranate molasses, fermented turnip juices, chilli, parsley and mint, which almost pickles the onion as it is absorbed; I often go there just to eat it. The same white onions turn up as part of the salad array of the standard kebab shop alongside cabbage and shredded lettuce, chillies and the various sauces, but crucially in this case they are neither raw nor pickled nor cooked. They are rather, for want of a better word, massaged – as, come to think of it, is the cabbage.

If you simply shred a red cabbage and leave it in a bowl, the cut surfaces will soon dry out, and the whole thing will look tired and unappetizing; but if, instead, you toss it through with a little salt and massage it gently, working the abrasive salt into its flesh with your fingers, the cabbage will turn and remain a violent purple as the juices leach out, glistening with them as if freshly cut. A more heavy-handed version of this process, in fact, is the first stage of making sauerkraut, although the end result requires the additional factors of bacteria and time as well as the forceful application of salt. Do the same to an onion, which while containing if anything slightly less juice than a cabbage is composed of much weaker fibre, and the effect is even more remarkable; an entire bowlful of sprightly sliced onion, holding itself up in piles, reduces to perhaps a third of its volume, nestling in on itself as if you had cooked it, with the flavour equally transformed – even sweeter, and when lifted out of its juices, mellower, the biting allium acidity tempered rather than bolstered by the addition of good, coarse sumac, moist and dark. Leave it overnight and these combine to almost pickle the onion, but half an hour or so is perfect, leaving it with some structure and crunch.

This is not, of course, in any way a complete dish, but it is nonetheless a very useful recipe to have up your sleeve; since I learned the method it has become thoroughly entrenched in my repertoire, going into salads and salsas, sandwiches and wraps, or alongside any number of things. It would go well with the Çiğ Köfte on page 16, for example.

4 white-skinned onions
1 tbsp coarse sea salt
1 tsp sumac

Peel, halve and trim the onions, then slice them quite thinly into half-moons and place in a large bowl. It will seem like a lot of onions. Sprinkle over the salt and sumac and begin to mix and massage them in, concentrating on one area at a time until all the onion begins to soften and collapse. Leave for half an hour, then lift the onion out of its juices and into another, smaller bowl. It will keep reasonably overnight, although much changed, but beyond that the transformation is too much.

Salt-cured Cod and Nectarine

The story of cod is the story of salt; a tale of how this lumbering Nordic grazer was wrenched from Scandinavian waters, buried in beaches or lashed to racks and left to dry, covered in refined salt or simply in the biting sea wind, then taken by its sea-faring creators to what were the ends of their Earth, becoming on the way a staple of the cuisines of southern France, Portugal, Spain and Italy, joining the little darting fishes of their own waters. It is a story of trade and of movement, of the giant blonde Varangian Guards of the court at Byzantium and of the hard-nosed traders of Venice; a reminder that while we think food is a product of place and of the soil, more often it is a product of motion across the Earth and the face of the water. It is not a story I intend to tell here. Firstly, I am a cook and not a historian, and whatever story I told you about cod would not be a product of my own knowledge and research but rather a regurgitated précis of, probably, the work of Mark Kurlansky, who has written an excellent biography of the fish; secondly, it is not especially relevant to the subject at hand. This ancient method of salting cod, seeing it almost desiccated into a wood-hard mass in a manner closer to the manufacture of dried meats than to conventionally cured fish, is not by and large one intended to take the place of cooking, being chiefly a method of storage which has taken on a culinary role. You could say this, of course, about many such products, but where those have mainly been adapted with modern techniques and technologies to be ready-to-eat, a fillet of salt cod or stockfish, taken as they are, remains resolutely inedible.

In Messina, in north-east Sicily, so close to the mainland but worlds apart, they say that there are three constants in life: the sirocco, misfortune, and stockfish – which says more than I can about the place of cod in the Mediterranean kitchen. Certainly to the modern cook these fillets seem inconvenient, needing hours or days of soaking in regularly replenished water to soften and desalt their flesh, although in the La Boqueria market in Barcelona (and I'm sure elsewhere) beautiful market stalls of cool marble and running water sell bacalao at different precise stages of rehydration; the one thing nobody seems to have now is time. Once thoroughly soaked, in any case, the fish is usually cooked. It might simply be poached and then pounded with olive oil, milk, bread or potato or just itself into one of the emulsified mixtures, slightly hairy from the dried fibres of fish, known variously as *brandade, brandada, baccalà mantecato, atascaburras* and probably a hundred other names; it might be made into *croquetas* or fritters, stewed in tomato sauce with olives, or baked under a layer of aioli to form a crust almost like the skin of a good rice pudding; it might be cooked with chickpeas or potatoes and peppers and onion, and it goes very well with egg – either topped with a soft-boiled egg or folded into an omelette – but it is, traditionally, cooked. There are exceptions to this and it is certainly possible to eat it raw, although the extra soaking it requires in order to do so – the cooking process obviously softening the fish as well as generally leaching some of the salt out – on top of the time already spent before you acquired it on salting and drying the fish, make the task as a whole exhausting just to think about. If you want to eat raw salted fish there are luckily quicker and more practical ways to go about it.

Salt cod, baccalà or bacalao is cured with salt, while stockfish (or *stoccafisso*) are cured simply in air; in Venice, with what seems to me a particularly Italian flourish, they use the terms the wrong way round, perfectly aware that they are doing so but refusing to change. What this confusion in any case demonstrates, is that the two products are largely interchangeable, with stockfish requiring just as long a soak to soften it as salt cod does to desalinate. As I understand the matter, stockfish is the original form, dried naturally in biting wind, with salt cod an adaptation for warmer climates; cod caught by far-ranging Basque fishermen could be salted on board to protect it for the journey home. Although stockfish is made with whole fish and salt cod with fillets, both are fully dried products, with the salt in the latter mainly there to protect the cut surfaces of the fish from harm as it dries. Neither can really be made at home. Stockfish gets its name from the huge wooden racks on which it is dried, facing out into the bracing northern seas. Once it has lost enough moisture to the wind it is moved indoors to be aged for up to a year. Salt cod, on the other hand, is dry-salted or brined until saturated with salt, matured for a few weeks, and then sold as it is or dried further to make the product shelf-stable even in hot weather, which would originally have been traded around the Mediterranean – called clipfish to distinguish it from the purely salted kind. Projects such as these require a particular combination of equipment, climate and very forgiving neighbours in order to carry off at home; even if you possess all of these I would still suggest that there are better uses of your time, and that if you wish to eat bacalao you simply buy good dried cod of whatever kind. Other and quicker forms of cured fish are quite another matter.

An endless stream of recipes abound – I have written some myself – for variations on the cured salmon known variously as gravlax or gravadlax. The name means 'buried salmon', or salmon in a grave, and refers to the practice I mentioned earlier of curing fish by burying it in saline environments such as cold beaches, the ground maintaining a steady temperature much like the kimchi pits of Korea and indeed the wine cellars of everywhere. Often what matters in curing is not so much precision as consistency. Be that as it may, gravadlax enjoys its popularity as a cured product you can make at home, due to its adaptation to the modern home kitchen – with the steady temperature provided by a refrigerator, the saline environment by a thick layer of salt and the burying often, but not necessarily, replicated with heavy weights on top of the fish. Tastes also change with technology, of course, and the salmon or sea trout, whether buried additionally in dill, beetroot or vodka, will generally be cured much less than its culinary ancestor under the cold sand, perhaps only for three days or so before slicing and eating. This is enough to recognisably change the flesh of the fish from its raw state, although not by any means to the softly flaking opacity of a fully cooked trout or salmon. If anything, it is a shift in the opposite direction, the fibres of muscle forming together into one mass, a brighter and more vivid iteration of its raw self. It is, I would imagine, quite unlike the original sand-fermented gravadlax, but I suppose this is how dishes change; something of the spirit remains.

A similar evolution has happened with salted cod, although as the product is still available in its original form perhaps it constitutes more of a divergence; it certainly adds to the confusion already caused by the proliferation of names for various kinds of cured codfish. This modern form, which I'll call salt-cured cod by way of differentiation, is peculiar in that while it is essentially a completely different product it is used in much the same ways as the traditional form and within the same cuisines, even the same dishes. Where salt cod is, as I have said, a dried and matured product, made to last over months or even years, salt-cured cod, like modern gravadlax, has a fairly short shelf life. Although it will certainly last longer than the fresh fish, the purpose of its salt cure is chiefly aesthetic rather than practical; the resulting cod still needs keeping in the fridge, and it still needs to be eaten reasonably soon after curing, but that does not mean it is unchanged. Rather, the simplicity of the process, removed from other complications such as fermentation, drying, pickling, sweetening or pressing, allows you to see clearly what salt can do on its own. This, in the absence of other factors, is really not much more than it was doing in our tomato salad, which is to say moving water around; drawing liquid from the flesh of the fish and seasoning it in exchange, leaving it firmer, dryer, altered. Although perhaps not as visually arresting as the difference between raw and cured trout or salmon, the difference is nonetheless marked – the fish compact where it once sprawled, the cut flesh with a pleasant and almost astringent graininess under the tongue. Moreover, the flesh of white fish being much more delicate than that of salmon, the process is much shorter; I would cure cod like this for no more than six or eight hours.

It is worth at this point considering the difference between white and so-called oily fish. White fish, like the whiter flesh of land animals and birds, is essentially muscle that has not worked very hard; lamb meat is paler than mutton, chicken is paler than pigeon, and cod, haddock, pollock, coley and hake, supported by the surrounding seas, moving with seemingly lazy flicks of their tails, are paler than everyone. Oily fish such as anchovies and herring are migratory, and need to move rapidly, in those beautiful murmurations you see on wildlife programmes, when they are under attack from apex predators such as sharks and tuna – swift-finned and agile, with meat as dark as blood. Somewhere in the middle are semi-oily fish like sea bream and sea bass (as the French have it, the wolf of the sea), smaller and firmer of flesh than cod and haddock, with enough bitter oils in them to ruin a fish stock if made with their bones. Different environments and different lifestyles give rise to different animals, of course, which in turn give rise to different ingredients and preparations, and different considerations for the cook.

Scallops, razor clams, squid, those beautiful red prawns and all the other vast array of shellfish aside, it is bream and bass that seem to me most popular for consuming raw, with British recipes, in particular for ceviche, frequently calling for one of the two. We cannot easily get hold of the fish South American ceviche would generally use, and perhaps our choice is influenced by Italian *crudo di pesce* – literally just raw fish and generally little more than that, dressed with a little lemon juice and very good olive oil, which can be any shellfish or fish so long as it is straight off the boat, but often seems to be one of the semi-oily kinds. Their use in these preparations is in any case unsurprising – their firm and fatty flesh is particularly suited to eating raw. Buy a nice gilt-head bream (named for the surprising stripe of gold across the bridge of its nose), fillet and skin and trim it, and your work in the matter is almost over; cut into slices or cubes and very lightly dressed, the meat is essentially perfect as it is, but it is also, outside of the romantic and probably imaginary fishing communities who breakfast every day on crudo of bream, extremely expensive. If you don't want to work, you need money; but luckily the reverse is also true. Cheaper fish just need more of an investment of time. Cod, and in particular the wildly overrated hake, have flesh that when in its raw state is soft and almost pappy; when slightly past their best or while spawning has depleted their strength you can smear the flakes of meat between your finger and thumb. A salt cure, even brief, gives them the firmness of a much more expensive fish. In more than one restaurant I have worked in, in fact, all the cod and hake we cooked received a light cure, of no more than an hour or so, which as well as seasoning the meat right through makes a huge difference to the way it behaves in the pan, the drier and firmer flesh forming a good brown crust and holding its shape when tossed and turned; if you have ever sworn at a piece of fish steaming rather than frying in the juices it is expelling into the pan, which stick and tear the flesh when you try to turn it, then I would strongly recommend you cure it in future. A sprinkling of salt and an hour in the fridge is all it takes, although once salted and rinsed it is best to leave it for a further few hours – or overnight – during which time it will cure a little further and develop the slight stickiness to the touch known as a pellicle, which if you were smoking the fish is what the smoke would stick to; it is the beginning of the protective layer that keeps cured flesh safe from harm.

This is not to say that to salt-cure cod in this way, whether briefly before cooking or a little longer to eat raw, is to attempt some kind of ersatz bream or bass; far from it. The curing rather focuses the fish and enables it to become a clearer version of itself, capable of holding its own in a jumble of strong flavours as well as speaking clearly enough to sit raw by itself on a plate, sliced thinly and dressed just with oil, lemon and pepper. You can use it in any recipe or preparation that would otherwise use salt cod or stockfish, although you might find the texture unsatisfying in baccalà mantecato compared to the real thing, lacking a certain density and creaminess. It is very good gently poached in a garlic-infused olive oil, tossed slightly warm with some green beans and black olives, and topped with mayonnaise or a boiled egg; add some potatoes and you have a kind of niçoise salad, the gently flaking texture of the seasoned fish a good substitute for tinned tuna. I like it best raw, though. You can serve it as simply as the classic Italian crudo, but it takes well to one or two strongly contrasting flavours, especially something sweet and acidic. During winter, one or another of the progressive abundance of citrus fruits sits best with it – mandarin or citron or blood orange or pomelo – while at the height of summer, a fat tomato, grated into a bowl to capture both flesh and juice, might be all that you want to dress it with. I am particularly fond of the following preparation, with its gentler acidity of fruit and fermentation and the sunny hues of the fruit. If you don't have time to make the fermented nectarines then you can just use fresh fruit if it is good and ripe, perhaps with a squeeze of lemon to balance the sweetness.

4 nectarines

30g coarse sea salt, plus enough for the nectarines (see below)

1 tbsp red pepper flakes

1 tsp chilli flakes, plus optional extra to serve

1 tbsp fennel seeds

1 tbsp kefir or live yoghurt

500g piece of neck-end cod fillet, skinned and pin-boned

olive oil

mint leaves, torn

First prepare the nectarines. Bring a large pan of water to the boil and cut a cross in the top of each fruit. Working in batches, dunk them into the boiling water for a minute at a time and then take out to cool. When they are cool enough to handle the skins should slip off quite easily.

Halve and stone the fruit over a bowl, then cut into chunks. Depending on their ripeness they may collapse quite a lot at this point, which is okay. Ideally you should have chunks of fruit swimming in juice. Weigh the pulp and juice, and calculate 2.5 per cent of its weight in salt. Add this to the bowl along with the red pepper flakes, chilli, fennel seeds and kefir or yoghurt. Mix well and then pack into a clean jar (the bacterial fermentation means you don't have to worry about sterilization) leaving a good couple of centimetres of space to allow for expansion. Leave at room temperature for three days (it should be starting to fizz and sour) then transfer to the fridge.

Sprinkle the cod all over with the 30g of salt, place in a non-reactive container (ceramic, plastic or stainless steel are all fine), cover and refrigerate for six hours. Rinse and return to the fridge, uncovered this time, for a couple more hours or overnight.

When the cod and nectarines are both ready, slice the fish thinly, place in a bowl and toss with the fermented fruit. Stir through the torn mint leaves and a glug of olive oil and arrange on a plate, pouring over all the juices. Sprinkle over a little extra red pepper flakes, if you want.

Instant Charcuterie

As our salt-cured cod makes clear, there are things we do to our ingredients that, although traditionally taking place over months or years, can with the aid of more recent techniques and technology be made to occur over a period of hours, in a way that is neither an imitation nor cheating, but merely different; this is something personally satisfying to me, as my own interest in the slower processes of food has always battled with my impatience. Although when I was growing up my mother did the majority of the cooking, my father, a laboratory technician by trade, would on occasion take over the kitchen for what seemed like deeply mysterious purposes, with huge pans of sweet malt or dark berries or vinegar simmering away, tubs and bottles crowned with bubbling tubes, and ranks of waiting jars. During these times we were banned from the kitchen which, given my history of sticking my fingers into hot liquids and under heavy weights 'to see what happened', is entirely reasonable but only compounded the mystery, as did the fact that nothing seemed to immediately result from these processes; all their products went onto high shelves or into dark corners or the disused rabbit hutch, to mature and store for some unimaginable time in the future. Most of them were in any case unsuitable for consumption by children. I gained a glimpse into this world when my father offered to help me with a recipe for ginger beer. I do not now, and did not then, especially like the taste of dried ginger in quantity, and most of my knowledge of the drink came from Enid Blyton. I do have a vague memory of reading, possibly in a Roald Dahl tale, that ginger beer made one capable of prodigious burping, and it was probably this, as well as the fact that the recipe I had, from *The Weird and Wonderful Cookbook*, was supposedly taken from a troll, that made me eager to make it.

The process seemed endless; we had first to make a starter of yeast, sugar and ginger (the so-called ginger bug), which took a day or so to get going, and then to make up the ginger beer itself, really just sugar water with ginger in it, to which we added our starter and then left to ferment, tightly sealed in bottles – dark brown ones with ceramic swing-top caps. I distinctly remember my mother telling me in response to a question about these bottles that a family friend, from whom we had in fact bought our house, had once tried to make beer in ordinary glass bottles like the ones fruit squash came in (I had forgotten until writing this that I once lived in a time before the universal dominance of plastic), all of which had exploded under the pressure of fermentation. I imagined our narrow kitchen a nightmare of whirling glass. Luckily my father's home-brewing meant we had a good supply of the correct sort, and after however long in them the ginger beer was ready to drink. As the recipe recommended, you keep some of the yeasty sediment back from each batch to use as the starter for the next, and the process would then begin all over again. Although our ginger beer was as fizzily belch-inducing as anyone could wish for, the fact remained that I didn't like it very much, the natural carbonation too raw beside that of commercial lemonade or even of my brother's SodaStream, and I think I got bored of it long before my father did.

Nonetheless, the idea that work in the kitchen could take place over days or even weeks had been planted, although it would be some time until it came to fruition. When some time later I became a professional cook, I gradually became drawn to these processes, moving from dishes that took minutes to those that took hours, then to ones that needed hanging overnight, marinating for days, pickling for weeks; perhaps another way of putting it is that I got more patient as I got older. This, combined with my sincere love of cured meats and my then firm, if misplaced, belief that if a thing was worth doing it was worth doing myself in a somewhat amateurish fashion, made it perhaps inevitable that I would eventually try making charcuterie. My first attempt at full-blown curing was with a whole bone-in leg from a hogget (a year-old sheep), two of which the restaurant had bought entire from a local farmer, which I first buried in salt in a terracotta planter and then hung, protected in one leg of a pair of tights, inside a mostly disused chimney for a few months, giving it a poke every now and again to check its progress. When I gave a little of the result to a charcutier friend of mine, she asked firstly why I had decided to begin with the most difficult and disaster-prone form of ham to make, and secondly what business I thought I had doing so successfully. Call it beginner's luck, or perhaps the particularly suitable microclimate of the chimney; I don't think I've made anything so good since.

During this time I was also trying a number of much quicker recipes for curing meat, some measured in weeks and some only in days. Alongside the ham I had some hogget salami hanging up – which turned out perfectly well, although if making them now I would add some pork fat to the much leaner sheep meat – and in the fridges I had a number of projects. The difference between these and air-dried hams of the traditional sort is much like that between our salt-cured cod and salt cod or stockfish; while the latter kind are altered and flavoured by time, air, enzymes, moulds and bacteria, the former, confined to the more or less sterile environment of the refrigerator, are altered only by salt and by the moisture it removes. Whereas with fish, however, the difference is mainly one of degree, curing meat on a smaller scale opens up other possibilities. A fish is a fish; a round fish like a cod or a hake has, apart from its cheeks and tongue, essentially two muscles, mirror images of each other, which make up its body. This is all there is of them to cure, whether you do so for hours or for months. Land animals, in comparison, are complicated things. The limbs and midsections, which make up the so-called 'primal cuts', are themselves made of many different muscles, pulling in different directions, which during the life of the animal are worked in very different ways. Even cuts that are treated as uniform, like the collar section of pork, which might be cut into steaks or cured as coppa, contain many different parts.

What this means for the curer is that while it is impossible to streamline, say, the making of prosciutto (or at least limits how far you can usefully do so), there are other smaller cuts you can turn your attention to, producing something that rather than an imitation of the larger forms is quite another thing. In fact, curing in the fridge allows you to cure pieces of meat that would be very difficult to cure otherwise, being too small or too lean to do so without their drying out too quickly and too much; chiefly, it allows you to cure fillets. These so-called 'prime cuts', which still sell for a premium and are often considered the best candidates for quick cooking or for eating raw, are ideal for brief curing. Fillet is muscle that does not do much work and it can, especially with beef fillet, verge on being too tender – almost melting in the mouth, which is not a quality I find particularly desirable in roast or grilled meats. Nobody wants to be chewing on their steak for hours to come, but some bite, some reminder of what you are eating, is something I find necessary; and given that this supposedly premium tenderness comes at the expense of rough and richer flavour in these apparently prized cuts, a fillet isn't, as I have said before, even good for eating raw. What else is there to do except cure it?

Fergus Henderson has in his first book a recipe for beef fillet cured first in sugar and salt, flavoured with a little rosemary, and then rubbed in pepper, which I think may be what first sparked my interest in this kind of quick curing – although I confess I have never followed the recipe. Like most of his brining and curing recipes, it uses an extraordinary amount of salt (a kilogram in total of curing mix), but the main expense is the meat itself. An entire fillet of good beef (and there is no point in attempting such a thing without good beef) costs a lot of money, far beyond the budgets of various kitchens I have worked in and generally beyond my own personal budget, at least in combination with the time and inclination to undertake such a project. I found the recipe intriguing, though, chiefly because it seemed so straightforward. Many books you read on curing meat and fish, often with an eccentrically ramshackle self-published feel to them and written by men you know have at least two sheds, hedge round the subject with so many qualifications and complications that the undertaking quickly comes to seem impossible. You need temperature control; you need humidity control; you need to be able to measure weight in micrograms; you need to butcher your own carcasses; and on top of all this is the constant reminder that your project might, for any one of a number of reasons, fail entirely, and your money and your time will be wasted.

Henderson, in comparison, is entirely straightforward. While the proportions of sugar and salt in his curing mix are weighed out, the beef is not, and if you don't have quite enough cure to cover it he just tells you to make some more; curing is up in three days, with no metric of weight loss or precise textural change to govern it. While this is partly the directness of his style, it is also to do with the nature of the curing method, relying only on salt and refrigeration, and with the speed of the process. The meat does not really have the time or the opportunity to go off, and so the cook does not need to be quite so precise as with traditional charcuterie. You are free under these circumstances to experiment a little more and, as the purpose of the salting is for taste and pleasure alone rather than preservation and storage, to play with different curing times, quantities of salt and sugar, and spices; even to use completely different meats. Henderson suggests in his recipe that the same cure can be applied to a fillet of venison, which is, among a number of distinguishing factors, significantly smaller than a fillet of beef. Even a red deer, the largest species we eat as venison in Britain, has nothing like the musculature of a cow; and roe, fallow and muntjac deer are even smaller. Chinese water deer, which you see in the flat wetlands of East Anglia, are the size of dogs. I forget whether this recipe suggested a different curing time if using venison, but it is clear that is should be much shorter than for beef; times for these transformative processes, as for cooking with heat, of course vary with size and with weight.

Venison fillet is in any case quite expensive, but the open-endedness of this recipe and the possibilities it offered encouraged me to try it with the other animals we commonly eat, namely pig and sheep; the pork fillet I spiced with chilli and paprika in the manner of the Spanish cured pork loin, the lamb, or rather hogget, I left unadorned, sitting in salt alone. Both were very good, I think, although the pork perhaps made you yearn a little for the real thing, accustomed as we are to eating the animal cured. The hogget, though, particularly impressed me, because the process, compared to those stockinged hams swinging in the chimney, was almost instant; the little fillets, only an inch or so across, cured almost overnight, and the result, although lacking the deeper flavours that come with age, was like the real thing, the meat deepened in colour and drier in texture – as cured food should be, a more expressive version of itself. If I am no more patient in the kitchen now than I was with that endless procession of ginger beer, then at least I can keep myself distracted with little morsels like this while the fish cure, the pickles pickle and the larger charcuterie ages, thankful for the forceful work of salt.

You can serve this with anything you like to serve cured meat with: some cornichons and a dab of mustard, folds of salted turnip, a remoulade of kohlrabi or a jar of pickled onions found in the back of the cupboard. In the heat of midsummer, though, I like to serve it with something a little fresher. This pesto, called *marò* or *pesto di fave*, is from Liguria and traditionally accompanies white fish; but broad beans and peas both also go extremely well with lamb, summer children that they are, and mint and pecorino go without saying.

20g coarse sea salt
30g caster sugar
500g of lamb pencil fillets
1 tsp fennel seeds
1 tsp black peppercorns
1kg broad beans in their pods
1 clove of garlic
15g pecorino, grated
a small bunch of mint, leaves picked
50ml olive oil
juice of ½ a lemon

Mix together the salt and sugar and sprinkle around half of it across the bottom of a non-reactive container. Place the fillets on top and sprinkle over the rest of the mixture, making sure that all of the flesh is covered and any excess curing mix is heaped up around the fillets. Cover and refrigerate for twenty-four hours, then rinse and dry the fillets.

Lightly toast the fennel seeds and peppercorns in separate pans, then grind together in a mortar or spice grinder and lay out on a plate to cool down. Roll the dried fillets in the cooled spice mixture and then cover and refrigerate until you want to eat them. As this is not a particularly long cure, they will last not more than a week, firming up a little more in that time.

To make the pesto you will need to double-pod the broad beans, first removing their padded jackets and then peeling them out of their tighter shells. In midsummer your beans should be sweet enough to eat raw; if you find them a little floury, you can blanch them for a minute in salted boiling water, then drain and cool completely before making the pesto.

You can either use a food processor or a mortar and pestle to make the pesto. If using a food processor, you will need to crush the garlic completely with the side of your knife or grate it on a Microplane before adding it to the bowl; if using a mortar you can chop it roughly and then crush it in the bowl with some salt. Either way, add the beans to the crushed garlic with 100ml cold water and reduce to a coarse paste. Stir in the cheese, mint and olive oil and season with salt, pepper and a squeeze of lemon juice. If not using straight away, cover the surface directly with cling film so it doesn't oxidize.

Slice the cured meat and arrange on a plate, with the pesto and some bread alongside.

Raw Pork and Fig Leaves

Figs are deeply mysterious things, and if it is they rather than pomegranates that Eve and Adam stole then you can see why Jahweh chose the fruit as his repository for hidden knowledge; they curl their beauty inside themselves, the coarse black or green skin hiding fleshy, scarlet flowers. Nor does greater knowledge and understanding lessen the seemingly mythic potential of the fig. A year or so ago I read one of those articles *The New Yorker* magazine is especially good at, that expound with a certain breathless enthusiasm a more or less obscure topic in easily understandable terms and with a winning narrative drive, which explained that there are hundreds of varieties of fig tree, and that each is pollinated and populated by a different species of tiny wasp, fruit and insect remaining loyal to each other across the centuries, the eggs of one nestling inside the ovaries of the other. In fact, the wasps will often die inside the fruit, stripped of their wings on their way out, and for this reason, shortly after the article came out, some vegan activists decided that the fig was forbidden to those following a plant-based diet, which I suppose raises certain questions about insect and other life in the vegetables we eat. I do not know whether the Jain religion, whose monks and nuns refuse tubers and bulbs to save the insects harmed when they are uprooted and who sweep the ground before them so they tread on no living thing, forbids its adherents figs. The question of how much agency we can be said to have in such cases, and indeed of whether it matters if we eat something already dead, could be debated each way until the end of time.

The fig, in any case, is at least as mysterious in the kitchen as it is in the annals of science and religion. It is extremely hard to get hold of a really good fig in Britain. They are originally tropical plants, and although they grow well seemingly everywhere they do require lengthy heat to produce their best fruit. As when perfectly ripe the figs almost burst to the touch, and as the heady aroma of the sap begins to die as soon as it is cut from the tree, they do not travel very well. A fig in Britain tends to disappoint. It is mainly for this reason, I suppose, that it has become common in the last few years to infuse the flavour into creams, ice creams, aperitif wines, vinegars and fermented soft drinks – not from the fruit, however, but instead from the leaf, which grows in heavy abundance wherever the tree has a foothold. Although sharing some of the distinct flavour of the slightly unripe fig, the leaves have a flavour all of their own, much of it coming from the same sticky sap that oozes from the stalk of the cut fruit. Redolent also of coconut, the scent of the leaves on the hottest days is almost obscenely overpowering, too feverishly strong for the more delicate sensibilities of an English summer; they are one of my favourite ingredients.

A few years ago, when making a fig-leaf ice cream with perhaps a little less attention than I should have been, I think I must have overheated the milk with the leaves in it, or maybe the milk was a little old to begin with; whatever the cause, the result the next morning rather than a beautifully infused milk was a mess – lumps of jellyish curd coagulated around the leaves, which otherwise seemed to be sitting in a thin whey. This was of course very interesting – although I did have to take fig-leaf ice cream off the menu that hot summer's day. A very little research soon threw up the use of fig sap as a vegetable rennet – that is, as a curdling agent in the preliminary stages of making cheese. Traditionally achieved with an enzyme found in the stomach of milk-fed animals, but more usually these days with either a laboratory-grown or a fully synthetic version, it can also be done with tinctures of different plants, most commonly artichokes and other thistles, nettles and figs. I have since eaten a soft goat's cheese called 'ficu', made in Sicily by Giacomo Gatti, that is coagulated with fig sap and aged in a fig leaf; a truly remarkable cheese, but as at the time I was mainly concerned with not messing up my future ice cream and my fig leaves were mainly spoken for, I didn't do much experimentation in the matter. I did read some time afterwards in Sandor Katz's *The Art of Fermentation* that some people claim milk kefir grains can be grown by coagulating milk with fig leaves, but as kefir grains are among the odder bacterial cultures used in food, and especially as a leading scientist working on them has said (also cited by Katz) that we can no more make our own than we can put together a functioning cat from its constituent parts, I consider this unlikely.

Whatever the facts of the matter, the fig leaf clearly carries a great deal of potential, both in its use as an ingredient with a powerfully unique flavour, and as an agent for change. When I tried Gatti's cheese I had assumed that the leaf wrapping was there solely for flavour and perhaps a little for its decorative purposes, or to signal to the eater the taste of the contents in the same way that a sprinkling of fresh herbs brings the flavour of those herbs within the dish to the front of the mind; it was not until quite recently, while putting together the recipes and notes for this book, that I realised that it was perhaps performing a purpose of its own. It was not cheese, in fact, that brought this to mind, but rather in the course of a conversation I was having about raw preparations of meat, when the food writer MiMi Aye pointed me in the direction of a Vietnamese dish called *nem chua*, a sort of raw, pickled pork meatball. While researching this, I in turn read of a pork sausage called variously *som moo*, *naem*, *chin som* and *mu som*, which is distinguished from the more familiar sort by being both raw and contained not within intestines of any kind but rather in various kinds of leaves – including fig leaves. Where both traditional sausage skins and modern synthetic varieties both act in a passive way, serving as a container for the meat as well as a breathable barrier to the outside world that allows for the moisture loss required for ageing while keeping out unwanted wildlife, fig and other leaves take an active role in the process. The particular acids and enzymes within them that, for example, allow them to curdle milk, essentially allows for fermentation without ageing – a sort of short-cut to the lengthier and more complicated process of making salami.

Our fig-leaf sausages are relatively straightforward, despite relying on the mysterious workings of those leaves. They do not need the complicated interplay of bacteria and time that gives most charcuterie its particular flavours, perhaps displaying their tropical origins. To make charcuterie in the European manner you need access to somewhere cool and dark, where the air can circulate, not too humid and not too drying, with caves, roomy attics and cellars all being suitable. This is not to make the charcuterie 'safe' as such – the salt, and in some cases the bacteria, largely take care of that – but rather to keep the process as slow as possible, to let the meat breathe and relax without drying out too quickly, and to let moulds and yeasts take hold and bring with them their almost infinite palette of flavours. Som moo, in comparison, is almost instant – which is to say the process takes around three days – and, protected by its fig leaf, can pickle entirely at a very warm room temperature; people like to talk about food as a product of the land, but to my mind not enough attention is given to the weather. Think, for example, of the different solutions to storing milk represented by yoghurt and cheese, the former available in an endless cycle and ready after one day at a warm temperature, the latter needing a process of ageing and nurturing. Think again of the difference between, say, Turkish cheeses, matured in heavy brines or in goatskin, and the cheeses of Northern Europe, born in caves of bacteria and mould. So much of what humans are capable of is determined simply by how hot it is at any given moment. While it is in any case perfectly possible, assuming you live in a fairly temperate climate, to make European-style cured sausages in the confines of your own home (as in fact I will describe later), this recipe is quicker and simpler – and does not require you to leave raw meat hanging for weeks from your ceiling in a way that might disturb whomever you share your home with, an important consideration in any recipe.

You need to get good-quality pork for this, which you'll need to go to a butcher for. It should be a heavy pink, almost dark, and preferably aged so it is not too wet. Explain to your butcher that you are going to eat it raw, and ideally get them to mince it for you to order. If this isn't possible then I would suggest using good beef mince rather than inferior pork. Many recipes for som moo and its variants include cooked sticky rice, the sugars of which provide food for bacteria and therefore act as a catalyst for a brief fermentation. This is only necessary if you are using plastic or other wrappers rather than the leaves, the contribution of which makes the additional sugar unnecessary. Fig leaves should be easy enough to find; you may well know someone personally who has a fig tree and wouldn't mind you taking a few. If not, then next time you are walking around a town of any size, keep your eyes and your nose open; when the sun is out the smell of a fig tree sits thick in the air, a heavy, honeyed perfume that speaks of hotter, lazier days in the broad green shade of the bright leaves.

> *500g very lean pork, minced by your butcher*
> *10g coarse sea salt*
> *1 clove of garlic, crushed*
> *1 tbsp red pepper flakes*
> *1 red chilli, deseeded and sliced into long strips*
> *around 6 fig leaves, about the size of your hand*

Place the pork mince in a bowl then begin to knead it. You are looking to break down the meat and emulsify it with the fat, to make it more open to absorbing the seasoning when it is added, so really push and knead it for a good five minutes. You should see a noticeable change in the meat as it loses the texture of the grinder.

Add the salt, garlic and red pepper flakes and knead for another five minutes until really well mixed and sticky. Put the mixture in the fridge for ten minutes or so to cool down, and then take it out for a final knead. If you feel like a rest now, put it back into the fridge until you are ready to use it.

Lay a double layer of clingfilm, around 30cm long, on your work surface, and arrange the fig leaves on this with their stem ends alternating up and down, overlapping so as to form a continuous bed. Place the pork mixture along this and lay the strips of fresh chilli down the centre of it, then roll the meat around the chilli into a rough sausage.

Using the clingfilm to help you, roll the leaves up around the meat, tucking in the sides as you go and the top round and behind the meat, then wrap the clingfilm tightly around the resulting sausage.

Place this on a tray and leave to ferment at room temperature, preferably somewhere warm and reasonably dark, for around five days. When they are ready, the sausage should have taken on a kind of cooked texture; if you give it a prod it will begin to feel tougher and less like a roll of raw mince. At this point, you can unroll and taste it; the meat should be pleasantly sour.

Keep the fermented sausages in the fridge for up to a week. It can be eaten as is or grilled slowly in or out of its wrappings; I prefer to eat it raw, to enjoy the texture and taste of change.

ON SOURING

The transformations we have made so far to food are significant, the ingredients becoming totally changed – arguably, however, not so much as if they were cooked. A tomato leaking its juices into a bowl is altered of course, but not half so much as a tomato cut across its middle and seasoned with oregano, garlic and oil as well as salt and pepper and roasted in a slow oven for an hour or more into sweet and savoury collapse; this is undeniable, but the alteration of each is irreversible. A daube of beef hanger steak, unbrowned but stewed nonetheless into a dark and sticky mass is certainly more cooked (which is to say more altered) than the same cut charred briefly over smoking coal, but that doesn't mean that the latter is raw – and in fact I would add that you need the one to understand the other. Lacking the climate and the tools to make stockfish, we can learn a lot by reversing the historical development and starting with our salt-cured cod. Similarly, understanding the ways we use force and salt in (and outside) the kitchen, although their effects thus far seem minimal, allows us to properly understand what happens in the more involved processes of cooking that take place across the culinary world, especially when you introduce an element that the recipes have so far kept to a minimum – time.

It is true that a multi-day preparation process, beyond the scope of many recipes, would already appear to have time, as it were, on its side; but really, the overnight cure of the lamb fillet or the three days required for the pork and fig leaves are not processes of ageing; they are simply the time required for the initial process, whether of salting or of acidifying, to take place. You wouldn't say that even a whole pit-roasted pig, buried in the hot ashes of a dying fire for twenty-four hours or more, was 'aged' as such; it is simply cooked, for the length of time required to cook it. This is in contrast to many culinary practices which, after an initial attack of salt, of force, of acid or even of heat, need a separate period of maturation – of simply allowing time to do its slow work. This is the difference between our salt-cured cod and clipfish. It is not even a question of the length of time required. If you were to make your own hot-smoked mackerel at home, then after curing it briefly in sugar and salt and letting the skin dry to a pellicle, you would smoke the fish directly over smouldering woodchips, or perhaps rice and tea, for only twenty minutes or so; crucially, having done so, you would then allow it to rest overnight. This is a question of practice and not of degree. The whole process from start to finish might have taken less time than cooking that pit-roasted pig, or even a barbecued brisket in the Texan style, but nonetheless it has utilized time in a way those others do not; its final product is aged. Once again we find the crucial step is in leaving our ingredient well alone.

Sourness is one of our palate's essential tastes, and it is one I can remember particularly enjoying for almost my entire life, although I'm sure as a baby I would have had the same nose-wrinkling disgust at biting down upon a lemon as anyone else. Salt and vinegar crisps and Discos; pickled onion Space Invaders or Monster Munch; mouth-scouring pear drops with their nail-polish tang; sour Skittles and the short-lived lemon Polo; the yellow or green flavours, tangentially related to citrus, of any tubular sweet; my adult self has not travelled so far from this. If you prefer the more wholesome fare expected from a food writer, then let me tell you of my father's pickled shallots. Once a year, every year, when he had harvested the entire crop of shallots (the little round ones rather than the banana shallot more widespread now), which he grew and still in fact grows on the allotment a few minutes' walk from our house, he would set to work, first peeling them directly from the wheelbarrow in the back garden, a process that I have fond memories of helping with, sitting in the declining sun of the second half of the summer as the birds above wheeled and squeed; sometimes our neighbour's fancy pigeons would burst up from his garden in a great cooing cloud. In reality, I am sure, I would peel one, or at most three, before getting bored and running off to do something else. Once the shallots were peeled I knew they had to be immersed in brine for some unimaginable length of time, maybe a day or two, and then again in a spiced vinegar, apparently forever. There was no point getting attached to the shallots now, or the anticipation would have killed me. Once, in fact, I couldn't wait, and sneaking one of the jars down from the shelf above the stairs reserved still for alcohol, pickles and Halloween chocolates, ate around half of the contents before returning it to its place; my reward was the stomachache you would expect from eating several hundred grams of essentially raw onion.

It is to my credit, I feel, that I did not allow this unpleasant experience to put me off pickles altogether, and if anything I came to appreciate them more. I would further stretch the shallots, which in theory at least would see us through a winter of cheese-eating to make it to the New Year tea, by consuming also their spiced liquor, pouring a shot or two over a buttered oatcake in a shallow saucer, in a manner not unlike the various stale-bread soups of the poorer Mediterranean, which themselves have always seemed to me to echo something of the Eucharist. An Italian customer at a restaurant I used to work for once told me, apropos of nothing in particular, of a dish of stewed pigeon and layered stale bread that one would season at the table with a little wine, straight from the glass; I forget the exact details, and in any case they're not relevant here. The wine he described was sour in its way, but not like the sourness of a British pickle, harsh with strong vinegar and the tang of allium, and its purpose was not to transform but only to season. As with salt, however, these twin purposes of sourness bleed often one into the other. In modern British cooking, heavily influenced by that of often-imaginary sunnier climes, fresh lemon has largely supplanted vinegar as a supplier of sour seasoning, which is perhaps a shame. The latter, at least in the form of 'non-brewed condiment', is still the mainstay of the chip shop and the greasy spoon, and oysters are as likely to be served with vinegar, whether in the form of mignonette or as a component of Tabasco, as they are with a wedge of lemon; but in most cases the bright exoticism of citrus has won out. It is true that very little lifts a dish, whether of slow-cooked meat or seafood or of freshly boiled vegetables, like a squeezing of lemon juice – Giacomo Castelvetro, I was intrigued to note, generally recommends the juice of bitter oranges where the modern European cook would use lemon, although whether this was the fashion in Italy at the time or simply due to what was available in England is unclear – but vinegar, derived from a variety of sources in a variety of ways, is capable of great complexity, from the harshness of spirit and malt varieties to the sweetness of sherry and the rice vinegars of China and Japan, as well as aged products like the now-ubiquitous balsamic. In any case, all kinds of both citrus and vinegar are capable of transforming as well as seasoning.

The various acidities of fruits and ants aside, sourness is something that often comes with time; to put it another way, it is something we often associate with rot. Most of the things you can do with milk involve leaving it to 'turn', as the euphemism goes, with cottage cheese, kefir, yoghurt, *viili*, quark and so on all examples of death's potential, which finds its fullest expression in hard cheeses – the corpse of milk, as Joyce would have it – aged for months or years in caves, cellars, sheds and barns. The word 'vinegar' means rotten wine, which is indeed what it is, alcohol re-fermented by bacteria into something else, and it is capable, once aged, of lending this time to other things – of not just souring, but preserving in sourness, in a way fresh fruit juices cannot, at least without a great deal of help from other sources. Before sourness preserves, though, it alters, and it does so in a fashion remarkably similar to that of heat. On the one hand, cooking is complicated; the crust on that grilled piece of hanger is a collision of extreme heat with proteins and sugars, producing an effect very different from poaching a chunk of salt cod or stewing pigeons layered with bread. On the other hand, cooking is extremely simple. The protein-heavy products of animals are cooked when those proteins have coagulated – whether they have been scrambled or braised or fried – which is what all the various and vague instructions for judging whether something is cooked are really asking you to look for when you check the opacity, the resting give, the cleanliness of the skewer; the only complication is that they do so at very different temperatures that vary by type, by species, by age and by cut. Coagulated, they are both firmer and more friable, and aside from sterilization, this is the main purpose of cooking with heat – to soften and to break. As it happens, these two functions are performed perhaps equally well by sourness. Strong enough acids kill bacteria, of course, which is what we mean when we say they preserve; they do so arguably better than heat does, at least at the temperatures to which we usually subject food. Even much milder acids are capable of the 'cooking' part of cooking; through some process I do not entirely understand the juices of lemon, lime, bitter orange, sour apples and grapes or re-fermented wine, cider, beer and spirits coagulate and soften raw flesh into something that is not just 'cooked', with the coy quotation marks recipes for, say, ceviche always put around the word, but *cooked*.

Drunken Herring

Of all the different ways of cooking without heat that can be found across world cuisines, the one that seems most widely known within Britain and western Europe, or at least most widely appreciated as such, is ceviche. I cannot remember when or where I first ate this preparation, which is really just a quick way of pickling fish, or even when I last ate it, but in the past ten years or so it seems to have gone from a slightly risky oddity to the pages of popular cookery magazines, in the process becoming almost a generic menu term for anything sliced and dressed in the same way that carpaccio has. The classic Peruvian iteration is still a dish worth celebrating, with its chunks rather than slices of good, firm fish swimming in the pleasingly named tiger's milk that forms its marinade. Sliced onion, chilli and salt go into this, but the main ingredient is the citrus, either lime or bitter orange, which, as it saturates the fish, denatures its flesh in the same way that heat does, so the juices drawn out of it turn to a lactic opacity as they mix with the acid. Experts differ as to the origins of this dish. It would certainly seem that it predates the introduction of citrus to South America, which the conquistadors brought along with horses and treacherous death, the requisite sourness originally provided either naturally by equally acidic fruit or by the fermented juices of sweeter ones, but it is interesting that the name we use for the current South American iteration seems also to have been a Spanish import.

I was intrigued some years ago to come across a recipe for something called 'ceveach' in an eighteenth-century English cookbook I had bought cheaply second-hand, the title page and spine of which were missing. As I cannot now lay hands on this book, and in any case I never knew what it was called, the recipe is at present lost to me, but as I recall it involved cooking fillets of oily fish, perhaps mackerel, before immersing them in a marinade of vinegar seasoned and spiced with saffron and coriander – not untypical for a book with a much broader palate than one might expect, including, I remember, a variety of preparations of curry as well as a number of intriguing pickle recipes. The so-called ceveach, in other words, bore a strong resemblance not so much to the modern Peruvian dish as to the Spanish escabeche. This family of dishes, which appear also in areas of Italy once under Spanish control under the name *scapece*, is now most often made with fish, especially oily sardines and mackerel and various molluscs; traditionally the main ingredient might instead have been small game birds, such as the quail and partridge still loved in Spain, while in Italy you often find vegetable versions made with various kinds of squash. In any form, though, the dish consists of something cooked, generally by frying, and then drowned in a bath of sweet and salty vinegar, again spiced with saffron, alongside coriander, chilli or paprika in Spain; Italian versions tend to use less complicated spicing but use oil, onion or even breadcrumbs alongside the vinegar as the main preserving medium. Nowadays you can buy escabeche of mussels in tins (an excellent snack when tossed with a bag of crisps), whereas once a great slaughter of quails with net and gun would have preceded a hectic pickling, laying up barrels of the stuff for the winter.

Now, it is easy to see how a 'sc' gets elided and how a 'b' becomes a 'v' – the two sounds are in any case pretty much interchangeable, as I learned from a book on ventriloquism as a child. Much greater, to my mind, is the leap required to apply the word to a dish that is qualitatively very different, in that acidity is not used alongside heat to preserve a product but rather by itself as a method of cooking. In this sense, ceviche has less in common with the escabeche of the south than with the pickled fish of northern Europe, in particular the herring. Like the escabeche, of course, this is a method of preservation; herring, like sardines and mackerel, are a quick-moving oily fish, which once travelled in great flashing shoals across the depths of northern seas. Warming waters and intensive fishing have changed their habits but not their natures, and the so-called silver darlings still spoil as quickly as they ever did. The countries that fish them, in particular the Netherlands, Germany, Britain and Sweden, but also parts of Canada and Japan, have developed a hundred different ways to arrest this spoilage, from simply gutting and salting the herrings as they came onto the boat to more elaborate preparations of smoke and vinegar; even in Britain, where so many of our traditional recipes have been lost and abandoned, you can still find (alongside the more recent introductions from Eastern Europe with their dill and sour cream) the kipper, the Yarmouth bloater and, most relevantly to the current topic, the rollmop. Like the escabeche, this preparation is intended chiefly to preserve. Although now, as with every such thing, they are sold usually in plastic from the refrigerator, a rollmop, first salted and then immersed in its seasoned vinegar rolled around sliced onion, will last almost indefinitely in great barrels or jars kept in your pantry or warehouse or the depths of your ship; they are otherwise more like ceviche, however, as the fish are not cooked before their acidic bath, gaining their flaking texture and opaque flesh from the action of the vinegar alone.

Although rollmops have to my mind thoroughly entered the lexicon of British preserves, at least around the once-great herring-fishing centres of the east coast, the dish – or at least its name – is German in origin, alluding for some reason to a pug dog. This does not necessarily mean, however, that the rollmop is a direct and wholesale import from the Continent – although the waves of immigrants from the Netherlands to build the dykes and pumps of the Broads and to weave the fine silks of Norwich presumably brought with them some of their traditions. Rather, it is important to consider maritime communities not as living on the edges of their different countries, but rather around the boundaries of their collective sea, which for the sailor binds more than it separates, or in other words that the people of Yarmouth or Lowestoft have more in common with those of Amsterdam or Hamburg than perhaps they do with the people of London or even Norwich. This notion, which I think was first introduced to me by the writing of Robert Macfarlane and which merely requires you to look at the map in negative, as it were, makes the seemingly endless journeys of the Vikings as they traded and raided around Europe much easier to comprehend; they were not voyaging through many countries but rather around the edges of one entire sea, and taking their dried fish with them. Any seagoing community does the same, if not always with such impact as the Vikings, whose contribution to the food of the Mediterranean is arguably as great as that of the Columbian Exchange. Great ports in particular are always fascinating to eat your way around, finding a connection here and a dislocation here, seeing which parts of their cuisine look inwards to the hills and valleys and which out into the wider world, speaking not of the static weight of terroir but rather the bustling variety of human life.

Whatever the exact means of entry of the rollmop into British cuisine, pickled herrings of various kinds, but all with the defining feature of rawness, exist wherever people fish herring and also in many places they do not, the ease of storage and transportation of the preserved herring making it as popular for parts of the Catholic world as salt fish is in others; Poland, Ukraine and elsewhere have particularly taken to pickled herring for special feast days such as that on Christmas Eve. In most cases, we can infer that these various preparations are as much a product of parallel evolution as of direct influence and trade, with the influences of diverse food cultures and availability of ingredients making each iteration as subtly different from the next as it is uncannily similar. Vinegar, of course, is a constant, although there is a fascinating anomaly in the Dutch tradition of herring being only very lightly brined, fermenting in the enzymes of its own offal in the same way salted anchovies and fish sauce are produced (although for a much shorter period of time), a method that seems to speak of much wilder shores. The kind of vinegar varies as you might expect from place to place, along with the flavourings, which range from lingonberries in the north to sherry further south, usually meeting in the middle with such pickling constants as peppercorns, mustard, onions and bay leaves. Before pickling, the fish, generally in fillets but sometimes cut across in tranches (I have pickled herrings headless but whole, which takes a great deal longer for no discernible benefit) is salted, either dry or in brine, which essentially disinfects and slightly dehydrates the fish before the curing is completed in vinegar, which takes around a week to fully penetrate the flesh and cook it through. The recipe below is adapted from that of St. JOHN, and gives you a method that is safe and effective; if you keep the salting time and the vinegar the same you can add essentially whichever flavours you like, chilli and wild fennel dragging it one way, mustard and green peppercorns another. If you can't find fresh herring, then sardines or mackerel will do very well instead, with the latter taking probably a few days longer.

Sometimes, of course, the herring is only salted and then eaten as is, while often it is smoked instead of pickled, either hot and direct or more slowly through a system of pipes; I spent a long time considering whether to cover the practice, so vital a method of preservation and especially so to the herring, in this book, before deciding that even so-called cold smoking, which requires you to light a fire and is in any case impractical for the home cook without special equipment, could not really be considered a method of cooking without heat, despite its proximity to methods that are and the similar applications of its products. I will, however, add by way of an addendum that I was surprised to discover recently the popularity in Italy of the smoked herring, especially so in parallel with stockfish and clipfish in Sicily and in Venice; I had thought the silver darling, considered a poor man's food in comparison to once-luxurious cod, had never made it out of northern waters, but there they are, golden and huge in the fish market of Catania, considerably larger, in fact, than any I have seen elsewhere in Europe. In Sicily they serve the chopped fillets in a salad with chunks of orange, dressed only with olive oil and salt, the heat of the south colliding with this cold-fleshed immigrant, brought here who-knows-when on the giving sea.

100g coarse salt
300g caster sugar
8 herring fillets
350ml white wine vinegar
1 tsp black peppercorns
2 red onions, finely sliced into rings
2 celery sticks, finely sliced
1 carrot, peeled and finely sliced
2 bay leaves
a small bunch of dill

Mix together the salt and 200g of the sugar and layer this curing mix with the herring fillets in a plastic, glass or ceramic container, making sure they are covered by it both above and below. Cover and transfer to the fridge for twenty-four hours or up to thirty-six; anything more will give a very salty result.

Put the vinegar in a small pan with 150ml water, the remaining sugar and the peppercorns and bring to a boil, stirring to dissolve the sugar, then cool completely.

When the herrings are ready, rinse them thoroughly and pat them dry with a cloth, then layer them back into your cleaned container with the vegetables, bay leaves and dill and pour over the cooled pickling liquid. Cover again and keep refrigerated for a week; at the end of this time the flesh should be opaque and give to the touch as if cooked.

The herring will keep very well if immersed in their brine, but I usually eat them quite quickly, either as they are, chopped into potato salads or dressed with sour cream and pickled cucumber and eaten fridge-cold for a slightly wincing delight.

A Quick Sweet Pickle

While the flesh of fish and animals is perhaps where the transformation of sourness is most marked, the changes wrought by acidity upon vegetables are no less drastic. My father's shallots were not just marinating in that vinegar, waiting for the flavour to penetrate their surface; as I discovered from that stomachache, it was slowly leaching the rawness from them – too slowly, as far as I was concerned. Although my patience for such things is now considerably greater, and I am not often greedy enough to eat things when they are still effectively inedible, it is rare that I make such a pickle, requiring a lengthy series of different steps. Such practices require a routine that the shift work of the professional kitchen does not often allow in your home life. I would perhaps brine my shallots or baby onions and then, working an additional double shift to cover for an unwell colleague, lack the time or the energy to drain and to rinse them at the proper time and find that when I eventually did so the onions were over-brined and saturated with salt; a soak in fresh water might be the answer, in which case the reverse would happen and, a week later, I would discover a bucket of onions beginning to slimily ferment. I could have pickled them at work, of course, but there has been little call in the kitchens I have worked in for the bulletproof British pickle; malt vinegar, a few craft varieties aside, is all out of fashion, and a lighter pickle is the norm. Such pickles also have the advantage of being a lot quicker, which perhaps partly accounts for their popularity in the eternal now of the restaurant kitchen.

If you wish, you can pickle almost instantly. As you might expect, similar principles apply as to cooking quickly with heat, wherein the thinner the slice and the higher the temperature, the quicker the result; given that it is the acidity, and to an extent the salt, that is doing the cooking in a pickle, the solution is obvious: for the whole shallots, which despite their small size are uncut and entire, substitute thin slices; for the malt vinegar, which despite the strength of its colour and flavour is as weak in acidity as its parent ale is in alcohol, and is in any case generally watered down, use a good wine vinegar whose rounded depth belies its sharpness. The restaurant St. JOHN serves terrines and suchlike with a pile of sliced red onion and a little bowl of red wine vinegar alongside the essential cornichons, with the idea, essentially, that you pickle them yourself at the table. I have never tried this at the restaurant itself nor outside it, and despite the fact that as I write this I am only a few feet away from a red onion, a knife and a bottle of good wine vinegar, not red but a cloudy white, I have no particular intention of doing so now. I must confess myself a little sceptical. Even strong acid needs a short while to work. Taking only a little longer, anyone who has eaten in a bar or pub in Britain and perhaps elsewhere in the last ten years must be familiar with the pink pickled onion, which I used to make twice-daily before service, and sometimes again in the middle of a busier lunchtime. Sliced into rings or half-moons and immersed in pure white wine vinegar with a hefty amount of both salt and sugar, the harshness of a raw red onion is dispersed along with its delineation of colour into a sweet candy pink, all in the space of half an hour, ready to adorn your burger or your pulled pork bun, and contributing greatly I would imagine to the renewed souring of the British palate, which has aided the mainstreaming of the flavours of, for example, kombucha and natural wines.

In the course of this more complicated souring, the pink pickled onion, almost cartoonish in its colour and the exaggeration of its flavour, has perhaps fallen by the wayside, but it is still worth making if you find yourself otherwise pickle-less and in possession of grilled or slow-cooked meat, one of those non-recipes it is good to have up your sleeve, like the Roman quartet of pasta sauces or the proportions of your preferred cocktail. Just slice your onions in whatever direction you like, but in any case fairly thinly, and put them in a bowl with a hefty pinch of salt and a couple of teaspoons of sugar per onion, adding white wine vinegar to around half the height of the onion. Give everything a good toss and leave for about half an hour; they're ready when they are pleasingly pink and you can eat a slice without feeling the onset of heartburn. Given the ease and the speed of this process you may well wonder why anyone bothers taking any longer route to pickle, but the important thing to remember in this and in any similar recipe, is that the time you put into it reflects the time you get out. The violence done by the strength of the vinegar and the sheer quantity of salt combined with the structural damage done to the onion in the fineness of its slicing makes this a pickle only in flavour; it has no staying power, no possibility of ageing. Kept overnight in the fridge it will already have changed completely, and much longer than that will see it lose its texture and with it most of its charm. In this, as well as in its various uses, it is not unlike the kebab-shop onions we made earlier, with acid taking the place of force.

There is, of course, a middle ground between my father's shallots and the pink pickled onion – quite a lot of middle ground, in fact.

You can pickle at almost any speed you like. Quicker recipes, it's true, often involve the direct use of heat, which while strictly placing them beyond the pale of this book does aptly demonstrate the point that heat, acidity and time are to an extent interchangeable, with a lack of one requiring only a little more of another. I made recently a beetroot pickle, with inch-wide chunks of the striped Chioggia variety. Having brought my pickling liquor to a brisk boil, I cooked the beetroot in batches for eight minutes a batch, packing the chunks in jars and pouring the hot liquid over the top. The cooking, which continued gently inside the sealed jars, meant the result was ready to eat the next day, or really as soon as it had cooled down. Considerations of speed aside, I think I would always lightly cook chunks or thick slices of beetroot to be pickled in vinegar, as their fibrous woodiness does not soften easily without heat; the other option would be to shave them thinly on a mandoline and let that help you break them apart. In most other cases, however, the choice is yours to make and depends largely on whether the texture you want your pickle to have is more like that of the cooked or raw vegetable. Dense beetroot still keeps its crunch after the brief cooking, whereas it does not take much for a small onion to cook through to the middle, giving them a slipperiness I find unappealing in, for example, those Italian onions in balsamic you see in delis and on charcuterie boards. The Italian preparations of vegetables under vinegar or oil are more often cooked than not, with even thin slices of ripe courgette given a thirty-second dunk in boiling vinegar before being folded and packed into jars, which perhaps speaks more of an ancestral distrust of raw vegetables than anything else.

Cooking the vegetable directly in its pickling liquid or even separately in water is one way to add heat into the equation. Another is to put your raw vegetables and any of the more delicate aromats into a jar and pour the boiling liquid straight over them – a risky business if there is much in the way of chilli involved. This method, which used to seem to me an untidy compromise or even a betrayal of the proper (which is to say time-consuming) traditions of pickling, is now the one I use probably the most for vinegar pickling. The ambient heat seems more to kick-start the action of the vinegar than to cook the vegetables much itself, which in general – although depending of course on what you are pickling – keep a great deal of their raw snap. I especially like to pickle cauliflower – whether white or purple or Romanesco – like this in neatly halved florets; they take on a perfect texture and acidity overnight, losing the somewhat austere graininess of their raw self without taking on any of the aroma of boiled brassica.

If you spend much time talking to pickle enthusiasts, whether professional or amateur, or indeed whether of the vinegar-soaked variety currently under discussion or the brine-fermented sort we will come to later, you will soon find the discussion turning towards this issue of texture – and in particular the elusive issue of crunch, which after the obvious factor of acidity is perhaps the most important aspect of a pickle. The greatest difference between my father's shallots and any mass-produced pickled onion is not so much the taste, which in either case is chiefly that of industrial malt vinegar and a few spices, but the all-important texture. You should bite into a pickle with a coherent crunch very different from both the crumbling snap of an oatcake or cracker and the bite of the cheese it accompanies; supermarket pickled onions, in contrast, always seem to come apart in slightly giving layers as if cooked, presumably because they in fact are, heat-treated in the jars to sterilize and seal them. For some reason this does not seem to be a problem with pickled whole cucumbers of various sizes, from cornichons or cocktail pickles up to fully fledged gherkins, which of whatever brand or kind always seem in their industrial form to retain a perfect texture, especially when eaten straight from the refrigerated jar alongside a slice of appalling pâté; ironically, these are a particularly difficult challenge for the home pickler, faced with the problem of creating a uniform crunch out of thick warty skin and giving flesh, which turns easily to mush given too much acidity, too little salt or too high an ambient temperature. Contradictory advice abounds on the matter, as is often the case. The one universal I have found is the inclusion in the pickling liquid of some kind of leaf, whether vine, cherry, blackcurrant or oak, which apparently is due to some preservative effect of the tannins they contain, a bitterness working in opposition to the sour; when pickling in an urban environment, as is often the case, I have found a Yorkshire teabag works quite well.

The question of crunch dominates every aspect of pickling, but seems particularly relevant when it comes to the various shortcuts you can take with the degrees of cooking applied to your pickle. Clearly the more you cook your vegetables, the softer they will be, and it would therefore seem to follow that not cooking them at all – that is, pouring cold brine over them in their cold jars – would be the best method for maintaining crunch, but even this apparently logical conclusion is the matter of some debate. I have read it asserted –

and have in fact on more than one occasion asserted myself, despite having done no proper experimentation in the matter nor heard of anyone else doing so – that at least in some cases and with some vegetables it is best from a textural point of view to pour the brine over still hot, in fact straight off the boil, as I do with my cauliflower and with various mixed pickles. The sudden and immediate transformation of texture brought about by the shock of heat seems to last better than the slow one of sourness alone; as I have said, I have no real idea whether or not this is true. The difference, however, in a quick sweet pickle does seem to be negligible and it certainly speeds the process along very well. I would say in this case that the purism of a cold brine is misplaced and that convenience should occasionally be allowed to win out against some abstract sense of doing things properly. It is still the salt and the vinegar that enacts the transformation more than the heat, and the result is still a pickle; it doesn't entirely matter how you got there.

½ a red cabbage, roughly sliced
1 red onion, roughly sliced
6 baby turnips, quartered
a bunch of radishes, halved
450ml white wine vinegar
20g salt
50g sugar
1 tsp black peppercorns
1 bay leaf
1 tsp chilli flakes

Give the vegetables a good wash if you think they need it, then toss together and pack into a clean 1-litre preserving jar. Add the remaining ingredients to a large pan with 150ml water and bring to a boil. Simmer for a minute to infuse and then pour directly over the vegetables. Seal the jar and leave to cool, then store in the fridge for added crunch. The pickle is ready as soon as it is cold enough to enjoy, with salted boiled meat, cheese, or anything at all.

The Meat Goes Up

'That which is above is as that which is below', the perhaps apocryphal scroll of Hermes Trismegistus, the foundational text of alchemy, tells us – which, the mysticism of the rest of it notwithstanding, is as good a definition of the principles of science as any other. To put it another way, things are the same all over, which may or may not be a cause for celebration. In any case, this Hermetic maxim is a useful one for the alchemies of cooking, perhaps even more so when the guiding principle of heat is taken out of the equation; it tells us that we can extrapolate from our known ingredients and recipes to take in ones we have never before tried or seen, that flesh is flesh wherever it is found, whether in the wide blue sea or the high black skies. Consider for a moment learning how to perfectly cook a chicken breast – a piece of pure, muscular protein without the distractions of bones or fat. Whether browning it first in a pan and roasting it through in the oven or gently poaching it in barely quivering water, the process may seem of limited application in the wider world of offal and thighs and whole birds, let alone that of entirely different animals. However, it teaches you a great deal about what it means to cook and be cooked, how flesh should feel underneath your hands. Once you realize the universality of heat, the world of cooking opens up for you like a flower; if these notes demonstrate anything, I hope it is that the actions of salt, of force, of acid and of time are universal, too, and that any of these recipes can be subjected to ten thousand variations, swapping ingredient and seasoning to create something new.

Despite all this, we often seem reluctant (I include myself in this) to apply the lessons we have learnt across the animal kingdom, especially it seems when it comes to the sea, that marginal and alien domain that covers the majority of our planet. Especially in the UK, where we confine ourselves to eating a very small proportion of what can be fished off our shores, let alone from the rest of the world, a confusion and a mysticism surrounds the buying and preparation of fish and seafood, which is not found in the flesh of mammals and of birds. The recent adoption by British chefs of dry-ageing fish is something I have already discussed, with the now-obvious idea that what works for one meat will work for another obfuscated by the cult of freshness that surrounds the consumption of aquatic animals of all kinds; taking this further into the idea of fish charcuterie seems, on the basis of my own personal experiences, to fill people with horror. Partly I think this is simply a fear of the unknown. Tinned tuna, salted and then packed and cooked under oil, is a preserve very similar to the duck legs of Gascony, and any disgust caused by it is probably caused more by a lingering and unjustified horror of mayonnaise and sweetcorn than any trepidation at the process or product itself. Caviar, bottarga and taramasalata, even in its pink-dyed supermarket form, are all applications of the same principles of curing we apply to land animals, and with the twin draws of sophistication and holiday nostalgia are accepted reasonably widely. Start talking about dry-cured tuna sperm, on the other hand, and nobody wants to know. I had this recently, in fact, in a restaurant in Trapani and the waiter refused to tell me what it was until after I had eaten it, fearing my visceral disgust would get in the way of my enjoyment. As it turned out, it was ridiculously over-salted and therefore disgusting for quite another reason, which was a shame. The cured tuna loin, on the other hand, a delicacy also in parts of Spain, was delicious – a match for any pork charcuterie you might name, without any of the strange metallic tang aged fish can take on. Much of East Asian cuisine, of course, rests on building blocks of cured and fermented fish, as did the cooking of classical Rome, which I will return to later.

Given this general mistrust, it is perhaps unsurprising that we do not often encounter the situation in reverse – that is to say, of the preparation methods of sea creatures applied to those of the land. There is nothing analogous to the popularity of sushi when it comes to the consumption of raw meat in the UK, for example, no supermarket carpaccio for the office luncher, no conveyer-belt purveyors of tartare and chips, however much I might wish for them. The supposedly delicate methods applied to fish are perhaps not considered enough to tame the stronger flesh of mammals. I cannot, for example, think of a dish in which pork or beef is pickled raw in vinegar in the manner of a rollmop; pickled meats in my experience might be either ready-to-eat products that have been cooked and sometimes matured in their vinegar – as the pickled trotter I had in a smoky restaurant in Tbilisi, in a sort of salad with coriander and fresh green chilli – or conversely pickled raw in vinegar but intended for cooking chiefly as a flavouring, like the 'pickle meat' of New Orleans. Confusingly, heavily brined cuts such as beef brisket and tongue or various cuts of pork, destined for a long poach or braise, are also sometimes referred to as pickled, especially in recipes of the United States, although it is also an older British usage now not really seen. I see no reason, though, why you could not make up a jar of cubed raw beef in spiced vinegar and wait for the sourness to cook it through.

It would take a little longer than the week that herring fillets require, I am sure, but the action in either case of sourness upon protein is the same. In Mexico a dish of beef is cooked with lime juice in the exact same manner as the tiger's milk of ceviche, the chief difference being that the denser and darker flesh of cows is more broken before its souring, being ground rather than cut into chunks.

This is often true of preparations of the uncooked meat of land animals, as we have already seen, from steak tartare in its various forms to the chopped and pounded sour pork of Vietnam; the beginner charcutier is often advised to start their apprenticeship with salamis rather than whole-muscle cures, an understandable if perhaps misguided position I will examine later. Simply put, and at the risk of labouring the point, this is because the skeletal muscle of land animals, and even of birds, is far denser than that of fish, which as we have already discussed is due to the support of the water that surrounds the fish. A piece of fish is quick to cook and quick to cure in comparison to a similarly sized piece of meat, and so it makes sense in some cases, especially without the backup of refrigeration, to cut the latter as finely as possible, significantly speeding the process of curing or souring and allowing it, therefore, to rapidly overtake the competing process of rot. This makes sense especially in the hot countries where such recipes prevail, but colder climates have always allowed for a little less caution in such matters – and refrigeration of course now means that we can all take advantage of this, even if not blessed with mountain or cold sea winds, caves or cellars, or convenient beaches in which to bury things. What this allows us do to is to follow recipes and techniques that are neither the instant cures and quick-soured dishes we have already looked at nor fully fledged charcuterie with its ambient ageing that allows for the wind-born attentions of bacteria and moulds. Rather, this effect can take place over a period of weeks entirely under refrigeration, allowing for a gentler use of salt and sourness than would otherwise be safe; a kind of whole-muscle pickled meat without overpowering acidity. In general, this involves the use as a souring agent not of vinegar but of wine.

Although not as purely sharp as its resulting vinegar, and although many people would see sourness in wine if expressed as such to be a defect, wine is certainly acidic, often more so than supposedly sour fermented drinks like kombucha and kefir; if we perceive it as less so it is firstly because different types of acid are involved and secondly because other flavours in wine balance out the acidity. This doesn't, of course, mean that they cancel out its chemical effects. Old recipes for braised meat, especially English and French, often take advantage of this fact, with coq au vin, for example, requiring you to marinade the old rooster with a bottle of wine, perhaps for several days, a process of tenderization not really necessary with the young and inactive animals generally available today. If, however, you follow one of these recipes to the letter, perhaps for a daube of beef or for some sort of ragout of game, you will find that after the marinating period the meat is not just stained a somewhat unpleasant purple, but also opaque on the surface and beginning to string apart, the acidity of the wine having begun to cook it. This can often, especially in very lean game animals, have the opposite of its intended effect and toughen the temperamental meat. As the winey bath also makes it very difficult to brown the meat before braising you don't see this technique very much in modern recipes, although I was given recently a technique for cooking porcupine by a Sicilian with whom I was staying that involved soaking the skinned animal in vinegar for a week. Having seen this same advice in recipes for fox and for badger I think this is more to do with removing or covering a lingering rankness than for the purposes of tenderness as such.

What this in any case demonstrates is that while you might wish for stronger vinegar to keep some meats safe or edible, it really takes only a gentle acidity to cook them; to get to the point, it shows that it is perfectly possible to pickle large pieces of meat in wine, with a result that sits in texture somewhere between cooked cured meats like ham and pastrami and their raw equivalents. A whole school of such recipes exists in the northern parts of Italy under the general name of *carne salada*, abbreviated often to *carne sala'*, but in any case meaning simply salted meat. When I first read of it, one article rendered the dialect as *carne salà*, meaning in Italian 'the meat goes up' and I spent some time trying to track down the story behind this name, which seems strangely appropriate for the sort-of-cure it receives, transformed without age and hanging, before realizing it was simply a mistake. In any case, the understated shrug of carne salada demonstrates, I think, that it is not considered charcuterie as such, its preparation being really only an exaggerated seasoning, but it also belies the complexity of its flavourings. Unlike, say, prosciutto, which as long as you ignore the effects of time and of microbial life is really made only from salt and meat, carne salada is heavily spiced with such northern flavourings as juniper and nutmeg alongside black pepper, bay, garlic, sage and rosemary, although not necessarily all at once; these might be mixed together with the salt and applied dry as a cure or in a brine, with wine added later in the process, or mixed directly with wine from the start for a more thorough pickle. Where this differs from the fig-cured pork of earlier, which after all is pickled in a fashion in the plant's mysterious juices, is in the degree of transformation. Where the raw pork is still recognisably raw pork, you would be hard pressed in some cases to tell whether such pickled meats as carne salada were cooked or raw, their outer flesh flaking as though boiled, the inner a wine-dark red as if cooked perfectly rare. If you ever come across the Lombard version known as *malenca*, which is wet-cured and lightly smoked, then you should eat as much as you can; this version is not that, but it is a good pickled beef and well worth the time and space it takes in your fridge. Consider it practice for greater cures to come.

1 tsbp black peppercorns
1 tbsp mustard seeds
1 tbsp coriander seeds
50g coarse salt
150g caster sugar
½ nutmeg, grated
2 cloves of garlic, crushed
1kg beef topside
2 bay leaves
500ml cheap, unoaked white wine
olive oil, to serve

Toast the peppercorns, mustard seeds and coriander seeds in a dry frying pan until their aromas start to rise and then grind in a mortar and pestle or spice grinder. Mix together with the salt, sugar, nutmeg and garlic and rub all over the surface of the beef, making sure the curing mix gets into every nook and cranny. Place in a non-reactive container, tuck in the bay and pour over the wine – it doesn't matter if the meat isn't entirely submerged – then cover and refrigerate.

Leave for two weeks, turning the beef daily if you can, or at least every two days, so it is evenly bathed in the wine.

After the two weeks, remove the beef from the spent pickling liquid, rinse briefly and dry, then leave it uncovered in the fridge overnight to dry out a little.

Slice fairly thinly and dress with a little olive oil to eat. Any leftovers will last around a week in the fridge, wrapped in baking paper.

A Digression on Sour Milk

I would like to turn now to something that is in some ways a diversion from the practices looked at so far, which have been concerned with the treatment of vegetables, animals and fish, but not as yet much with the indirect products of these creatures – the sperm and blood and eggs and other secretions, which inspire equally dedication and disgust wherever they are consumed, but without which it is impossible really to talk about sourness, at least in the cuisines of Europe, the Caucasus, the Mediterranean and the Middle East, the most notable of which is milk. Of course, not every culture consumes milk past the age of weaning, and the disgust with which the practice is regarded in other parts of the world is well known, going hand in hand with the intolerance of lactose that is really humanity's birthright, diminished though it is in milk-eating cultures. Partly, I think, this disgust comes from the decay that is ever-present in even the freshest milk. Whether in a coolly tiled northern dairy or in the fetid Caucasian heat, wherever you have milk it must go sour, and to an extent the defining features of diverse cuisines are what, at that point, they do with it. Cheeses of all ages and kinds, yoghurt, kefir, crème fraîche, good cheesy butter, viili and skyr are all examples, diverse in outcome, of essentially the same thing – milk left to sour. Nowadays of course this chain of productive decay has been broken. The progress of milk is tampered with and controlled at every stage; it can be chilled instantly upon milking, and pasteurized, thermized, ultra-heat-treated or otherwise sterilized of its natural bacterial load, creating essentially a cooked product with a far longer shelf life than raw milk, especially in the case of the UHT milk popular in much of continental Europe, which maintains its arrested freshness for an alarmingly long time.

Now, it is without a doubt that the work of Louis Pasteur has been, in general, a benefit for mankind, and in any case I am not here to argue for rawness from a health perspective. That a raw-milk dairy I buy from recently had to start heat-treating their milk due to the presence of tuberculosis in some of their products tells you a lot about the dangers we have to a great extent removed from our food chain which once were ever-present; progress, despite the constant stream of evidence we see around us and in the news every day, is not entirely bad. Pasteur and his legacy have, however, contributed to a narrative in which sterilization is always good and bacteria should always be considered potentially bad, a simplistic approach to a very complicated subject, which has infected our relationship with microbial life to this day. We have thrown the bacteria out with the bathwater, with the result – through heat-treated products of whatever method – of a milk that does not even go off properly, that flatly rots where it should go sour. It is the lactic acid bacteria naturally present in raw milk, native and well-adapted to their environment, that if given their head and allowed to breed at body temperature (the temperature, of course, at which the milk comes out of the teat) will quickly feed upon sugars in the milk and excrete them as acid, in doing so (and also in their own unrestrained reproduction) creating an environment unfit for other bacteria. Off milk is safer than fresh milk when it is raw; it is also more interesting as an ingredient. Sour milk in fact used to be a kitchen staple.

I remember watching some time ago a competitive televised baking programme in which one of the contestants was making, without flash or flair, an apple pie to his grandmother's recipe; as the contestant himself was not young, with something of the air of a benevolent watchmaker (in fact, a fob chain hanging from his waistcoat protruded slightly from his apron) we can consider the recipe to have been at least three generations old, and who knows how long it had travelled before it got to his grandmother. The recipe and its method possessed a certain quality one might uncharitably call pedantic, insisting that as well as the butter in the pastry, the flour and even the rolling pin were to be heavily refrigerated before use; everybody knows that cold hands make good pastry, of course, and I find this logical, if single-minded, extrapolation from this fact rather admirable in its way. What really struck me, however, was the use as a binding agent for his pastry of not water or alcohol, which I am told binds like water without activating the gluten in the flour, but sour milk, which in the days before the rehabilitation of bacteria, when even drinking a pot of Actimel was somewhat eccentric, seemed almost transgressive. Who was this strange old man with his rotten milk? I recall the host, I think, equally intrigued and appalled, trying to fudge the issue by asking if he meant, surely, that he soured the milk with lemon juice or vinegar? 'Of course not,' the watchmaker replied, 'It is milk left to sour, it gives a lift and a flakiness to the pastry. It is what my grandmother did.' Presumably he had a direct link to a source of raw milk.

Really this is all a matter of semantics. Nobody bats an eyelid if you bake with buttermilk, which is especially prevalent in the cooking of the southern United States and most of the time is not even what it says it is. Buttermilk, properly speaking, is a slight misnomer, as it is the thin liquid left after the butter has been churned from cream; if anything it is de-buttered milk. It is not unlike whey in appearance, watery and chalky-white without its richening fats, but if you have churned your butter from raw or cultured cream then it is dense with bacteria, which if left to their own devices will sour and thicken it to something more resembling natural yoghurt, which is what you want to use for baking. By itself it gives the same flakiness and fermenting lift as the sour milk; it is often used in combination with baking powder, the effervescence of which is sparked by the acidity of the soured dairy. This method is particularly common in areas where it is too hot to rely on yeast. Buttermilk you buy in supermarkets, on the other hand, is a quite different product with similar uses. Generally speaking, it has nothing at all to do with butter but is skimmed milk, pasteurized and then artificially cultured with lactic acid bacteria so that it thickens and sours in the same way as the real thing. Essentially, in other words, it is just sour milk, hiding behind a misleading name and with uncertain wildness replicated in laboratory conditions. It is also, it should be said, rather more attractive to look at than naturally soured milk, being smooth and homogenous where the former is curdled, lumpy and split.

This smoothness is something that so-called buttermilk shares with all cultured milk products, whether pasteurized or raw – that is to say ones in which the natural bacteria are replaced or supplemented by the addition of a starter culture, which may have been grown artificially or arisen spontaneously. These take a variety of forms, but are often grouped unhelpfully together in English as 'yoghurt' or at least as types of yoghurt, presumably because it is the most familiar to us of these somewhat alien preparations, having been introduced to our popular cuisine a handful of decades ago rather than a handful of years. I can see that it is tempting to introduce a new foodstuff, or I suppose a new anything, by emphasizing what about it is familiar and known, but when the products are in fact diverse in both production method and outcome, and especially when no legal or professional framework exists around the names used, it serves only to confuse matters. The Finnish product viili, for example, is often described and sold as 'viili yoghurt', when really it bears no direct relation to the sour milk of the south; yoghurt culture solely consists of various bacteria, while viili gets its distinctive flavour also from yeasts, and in particular its bizarre texture from a kind of fungus, which coats the viili in a soft but surprisingly tough layer so that it holds together in a mass somewhat reminiscent of mucus; pour it onto a table and it will gloop out as one, leaving the pot clean. This, in my experience, is somewhat alarming if what you are expecting is yoghurt.

Yoghurt and viili are at least made using the same method, which goes by the charming name of backslopping. As with sourdough bread and ginger beer, a small amount of each batch is kept back to culture the next load of sour milk, although viili cultures at room temperature where yoghurt needs the heat of the body or of warmer climates, which is unsurprising when you consider their respective origins. When you read of people nurturing their generations-old yoghurt starters, or indeed sourdough mothers, this is really what they mean. Although the bacteria or yeasts and what they feed on have been replenished ten thousand times, their owners insist that some link remains to wherever the far-off original began, and perhaps they are right. Be that as it may, the kefir culture, which takes a completely different form, seems to me to have more of a claim to a longevity worthy of Methuselah. As I said before, nobody really knows where the strange little white grains come from and how they are born, the theory of the fig leaf seeming to have no particular basis in fact. Whatever their origins, once they start to feed all they can do is grow, often doubling in size during the one or two days they spend turning milk into kefir. The grains are then taken entire and put into each fresh batch; if you don't kill them, it seems they really will live forever. Besides the lactic acid bacteria essential to all of these sour milks, kefir, like kombucha, contains acetic acid bacteria and also various yeasts, and if left long enough will become fizzy and even slightly alcoholic under their influence. In its proper form it is both very complicated and very different from yoghurt, and it is a shame that much of what is sold as kefir is nothing of the sort, being made not with the eternal grains but rather with a freeze-dried and powdered culture that shares little of their diversity and nothing of their charm.

To return to our soured milk, whether warm from the cow or, if chilled, allowed to return to an ambient temperature (but in either case unpasteurized or otherwise treated and silently teeming with its souring bacteria), I see no reason why it should not be eaten or drunk in the same way as yoghurt and kefir, rather than simply used as an ingredient. In Britain at least we never seem to have developed much of a taste for this unaged, 'fresh' sourness, preferring our milk to go beyond thickening to a complete separation into curds and whey. This split is a result of increasing activity, and can in fact be replicated simply by adding vinegar or lemon; in its division of milk into water on the one hand and proteins and fats on the other it is comparable to the action of churning, with souring taking the place of force. You can see how these different substitutes for cooking can substitute also for each other. In any case, left like this, the sour milk, pre-digested, as it were, by the actions of bacteria, might be a suitable food for the poor, the elderly, the ill or the young, as it was for the unfortunate Miss Muffet, but it has rarely been considered so for anybody else; for that you have to do more to it. Often this might simply be straining the mixture, separating it into food for pigs and its more useful part, which might be called syr or quark or cottage cheese or simply curd cheese, resembling ricotta while being the product of a completely different process. Curd cheese, when made with good milk and seasoned appropriately to its use, is an excellent thing, with a clean and pleasing blandness shared by mozzarella. It is also, however, very useful as an ingredient; everywhere that such fresh farmhouse cheeses are made they are also cooked with.

Although, as I said, ricotta is a different (if superficially similar) product, being as the name suggests recooked from the vats of whey left over after the primary cheesemaking and not, in Italy, considered to be, properly speaking, cheese, you can learn much about what to do with fresh cheese from the ways that ricotta is used, especially in the scorched south. Fresh ricotta, still warm from its boiling and eaten unadorned, has been the shepherd's breakfast for thousands of years – it is what Polyphemus comforted himself with after Odysseus put his eye out, the movements of skimming and straining familiar enough to perform blind – and when it is good, made from the milk of well-fed beasts, it is very good indeed; I have heard it compared to sea urchin in its proteinous complexity. As fresh cheese or ricotta sits, incomplete as it is, it will continue to weep out whey, and for this reason is traditionally kept in a little basket designed for the purpose, once of wicker but now generally plastic, within which it can drain. After a day it will be suitable for crowning toast, for pasta and for dumplings, and after another it will be good for baking – each another stage in the life of milk. Its death as a fresh product, its souring and curdling, is not its end but rather the beginning of a new cycle, which could, with the additional forces of salt and of pressure, continue almost forever.

A Long, Slow Pickle

When I originally planned this book, the intention was for this section to be occupied by my father's aforementioned recipe for pickled shallots. Perhaps in point of fact the recipe was my mother's, although it is certainly my father I see brining his wheelbarrow of shallots, in the same yellow plastic buckets he uses at other times of the year for wine or for beer; I suppose the provenance does not really matter, as certainly neither of them came up with it. It came to them originally from a book of Marguerite Patten, a writer who seems to hover around the edges of the so-called British culinary revival, lacking the supposed hauteur of Elizabeth David, the hospitable witchery of Patience Gray or the anthropological rigour of Elisabeth Luard; Patten's chief objective in her long career as a food writer seems to have been to teach people how to cook, now a somewhat unfashionable goal. Be that as it may, this recipe, while an extremely simple and arguably unimprovable method for pickling shallots or small onions, is not one I have ever myself followed, or really had any more of a hand in than the half-hearted peeling of a few alliums in the calm of the back garden and then, months later, eating the results, and it would feel dishonest to set it down here as if I had pickled those onions a hundred times. In any case, I have already said about as much as I wish to about these family pickles; this is not intended to be a personal memoir.

On the other hand, the pickled onion in general is worth discussing, as it seems to me to be a perfect example of a manner of preservation that is if not strictly speaking unique, then certainly peculiar to the British Isles, this lengthy bath in vinegar. As we will see more thoroughly later, much of the world pickle their summer gluts in salt, whether added dry or as a brine, in high concentration to sterilize or in a lower to ferment. Entire culinary cultures, really, are built around this practice, from the ubiquitous kimchi in Korea to the fermented everything of the Faroe Islands, and in such cuisines, vinegar more frequently makes an appearance as a quick seasoning or condiment than as a lengthy preserving medium. Japan, for example, possesses extraordinary traditions both of pickled vegetables and of vinegar – the former preserved dry, in brine, in soy sauce and in lovingly prepared beds of bacteria and bran, the latter from a variety of alcohols and fruits – but it keeps them largely separate (though there are of course exceptions). Not everyone loves the tantalizing scents of salt and decay, I suppose, but nor does anyone else seem quite as enamoured of vinegar as are the British. Even the Sicilians, whose love for jolting combinations of sweet and sour and savoury is perhaps as pronounced, don't in general preserve things in vats of vinegar; the typical southern preserve, perhaps of artichokes or dense-fleshed courgette, is given only a brief and sterilizing dip in boiling vinegar before being drained and dried and packed in oil.

This might uncharitably be attributed to a certain British barbarism of the palate, a love of extreme flavours at odds with the Victorian reputation of our nursery and boarding-school cuisine, but seen in the use of ketchup and brown sauce as breakfast condiments, in the nose-searing heat of English mustard and horseradish, in the ready adoption of a generic 'curry' into our national cuisine, in the easy popularity of Cantonese takeaway food, and in the current vogue for ear-burning chilli sauces; or you might say that it is the development of the palate in a different direction. We can see the detail in things we love where others see blank space, and I think in any case it is foolish to try to attribute moral or aesthetic worth to such broad differences of approach. The tyranny of reductions and butter in a certain kind of French cooking, where everything tastes of veal jus and the meal as a whole leaves your lips shining with fat, is in its way as one-dimensional as a bowl of fried potatoes covered with ketchup; in fact, done badly it is more so. Sourness, I am trying to say, occupies a particular place in our cooking, with heat or without, and it is important to recognize the sourness of vinegar as distinct from the gentler acidity of lemon or of yoghurt, not only for how it tastes, but for what it can do.

We have already seen the changes vinegar will enact on the flesh of fish, changing raw homogeny to flaking edibility, as strong in its way as the glowing coals or simmering water that would usually do the job; it does so quickly enough that were you patient and tireless, you could sit and watch it happen; even lacking these qualities, it is easy to monitor the process. Take a fillet out once or twice a day and gently break it open, and you will see the sourness doing its gradual working, forming a ring of cooked flesh around the outside of the fish like that of a piece of rare beef. Do this too much, of course, and you will end up with a mush of broken and unevenly pickled fish. Although we might tend to think of vegetables in general as much more delicate than the animals of land or sea, lighter than flesh on the stomach and on the palate, they are mostly much more robust, and often require much more cooking; think how long it takes to grill a centimetre-thick slice of aubergine in comparison to a similar steak, or to roast a celeriac instead of a poussin. Multiply that by the time required to pickle, and what you have with even quite a small onion is a very slow process indeed, so slow that it seems not to be occurring at all, until you wake up one day several months down the line and find that you finally have something to go with your cheese. I cannot watch it happening, and so as a cook it is both mysterious and frustrating to me. There is nothing to grab hold of, no adjustment to be made midway through the process in order to feel that you are in some way involved in it – that it is something you are making rather than watching make itself; you have to let it go. Sometimes this is a matter of willed patience, and sometimes simply of forgetfulness.

The reward of this patience is, on occasion, a transformation beyond even what heat can do to food. Most of the preparations we have discussed so far are ones that in some fashion or another stand in for cooking, with the results to an extent interchangeable, the edibility of a fillet of herring or an onion similar whether it is tenderized by heat or by acid. The processes behind them, however, can in some cases do even more, making something good to eat out of an ingredient which in its natural form is foul or even poisonous to the tongue; this is the point where souring begins to tip over into ageing, and indeed where all our different processes begin to come together. A good example of this, already mentioned in the context of breaking, is the olive, most varieties of which are mildly toxic when raw and unprocessed and require a long period in salt or simply in water to leach out some of their mouth-itching bitterness before being seasoned and usually in some fashion pickled before they are suitable for eating (although even then of course as an acquired taste), the whole of which can take a year or more. Try a raw olive and you will see why the puckering tannins of sloes and wild plums have sometimes been considered an acceptable substitute; Frances Hill, in her 1744 work *Adam's Luxury and Eve's Cookery* gives a somewhat imprecise recipe to 'Pickle Plumbs [*sic*] Like Olives', while more recently the restaurant Craft has conducted similar experiments. Even a sloe, however, has nothing like the bitterness of an olive, and their pickling or salting takes nowhere near as long as the various traditional Mediterranean methods. As ever when I consider this lengthy process, I wonder why anyone bothered. The fruit of the olive was originally cultivated for oil production, which gives a far quicker result and is really much more useful in a general culinary way than a salted olive; quite why anyone would tie up their potential oil in the extended folly of curing the things is beyond me, although perhaps the answer is simply that they wanted to. Taste accounts for a lot.

If you ever get hold of a box of raw olives of whatever colour, and furthermore if you plan on living in the same place for most of the coming year, then I would guardedly recommend curing some for yourself. It is, it's true, immensely satisfying to get to the end of a year-long process with something good to show for it, especially when you remember the harshly unpromising fruit with which you began; but it is also immensely annoying if anything in the meantime goes wrong, as it quite readily does. The best possible result, in any case, is something indistinguishable from good cured olives bought from someone reputable. You can, of course, tailor the curing and the spicing to your own taste, but as the two main objections to olives – that they are bitter and that they are salty – are somewhat built into the product, there is only a certain amount of room for personal preferences, especially as olives are already readily available to buy in a huge array of varieties and associated seasonings. What's more, although raw olives are certainly cheap in comparison to cured ones, you need to take into account the salt and the oil you will pack them in… Perhaps, in fact, I wouldn't recommend curing them at all, unless you happen to have a number of olive trees and a suitable climate, in which case you probably know what to do with them already. For this long, slow pickle I would rather talk about something a little closer to home, which also happens to require rather less of an investment of time than a cured olive of whatever kind.

Perhaps because of an early association with Christmas, I think of the walnut as a very English nut, almost as much so as the squirrel-loved hazel and certainly much more so than the Brazil, the cashew or even the almond. In general, however, it would seem that we don't do a great deal with it; coffee cake and Walnut Whips of course, as well as simply eating them from the shell during the festive season, but compared to the glory of the walnut in the cuisines of Turkey, Armenia and Georgia, and no doubt elsewhere, where it might thicken sauces or provide their main component, or be candied whole or encased in a sort of grape-juice wax, we really make little of it. By way of compensation, I suppose, we have the pickled walnut, one of those almost-forgotten British preserves that has thankfully clawed its way back to the mainstream. I don't exactly recall when I first tried one of these, although I have a vague memory that my grandma kept a jar at the back of the fridge next to the pickled beetroot and the red cabbage, all three of which I found faintly alarming. I didn't, when younger – Christmas notwithstanding – particularly like regular walnuts, judging them to taste of earwax and look like brains, and the sight of them bobbing sinisterly in their black liquid didn't do much to endear them to me in their pickled form either; on top of this I think I found the whole thing confusing. How could you pickle a nut? A pickle should crunch, not splinter. It was some time before I discovered firstly that they were pickled while still soft and green and secondly that they were delicious, and a great deal longer before I worked out how to make them so.

Before a nut is a nut it is a strange kind of fruit, with a toughish skin that gives way inside almost to jelly, and the walnut in Britain is in this state really for quite a short period of time, for a few weeks when the sun beats down but before the green of the landscape begins to give way to gold, which is to say around the middle of July. When you go to harvest them you take with you, if some recipes are to be trusted, a knitting needle; if this cannot be easily pushed through the nut then that is it, you have missed your chance on pickled walnuts for the year, unless you can find a tree further north and earlier on in its yearly cycle. I suppose a knitting needle is considered the perfect point of sharpness, or rather bluntness, to perform an accurate test. If you can get a knitting needle through something then you can surely get your teeth through it. I tend, more practically, to use a pocket knife – not an especially sharp one, with the awareness that it needs to slide easily into the flesh of the future nut; any resistance means that it is probably too late, although you can always use slightly more mature nuts to make *nocino* liqueur. Now, all that this test proves is that you could physically eat the fruit you have in front of you. At this stage you most certainly would not want to. Like olives raw, walnuts at this point are extremely bitter, containing an enormous amount of black, tannic juices, which need soaking out before the process of souring can begin. Unlike those seemingly changeless shallots, this process, though long, is one you can watch happening, seeing the black ink billow out of the once-green fruit, clouding their liquor as they recede into the dark.

1.8kg green walnuts
400g sea salt
1.5 litres white wine vinegar
300g caster sugar
4 bay leaves
1 tbsp black peppercorns
1 tbsp mustard seeds
4 cloves

Cut the walnuts in half on the diagonal and pack into a sterilized jar. Make a brine by filling a pan with 2 litres water and half the salt, then heating gently until the salt dissolves completely. Leave to cool, then pour over the walnuts. Seal the jar and leave for a week.

Make up another batch of brine in the same way. Drain the walnuts, then rinse and drain again. Rinse out the jar and return the walnuts to it, pouring over the fresh, cold brine. Leave for another week.

Drain and rinse the walnuts again, then lay them out on drying racks or tea towels and leave somewhere warm and dry; full sun is ideal, but a warm room or a low oven will do if the weather is misbehaving. You want them to oxidize and become a uniform black, which will take a few hours in the oven or perhaps a day elsewhere.

Add the rest of the ingredients to a pan along with 500ml water, bring to a boil and simmer for five minutes. Leave to cool completely with the aromatics. Put the black walnuts back into a clean jar and pour over the cool pickling liquor. Leave to pickle for at least two months, out of sight and out of mind; they will be at their best for Christmas.

ON AGEING

As soon as any ingredient becomes an ingredient – which is to say from the moment we first break it, whether from the tree or from its waking life – it begins to decay. Most of the story of human cuisine, and therefore of civilization, is the attempt to arrest this process, to take the abundance we have when the land is fat and the sun is hot and keep it safe for darker times. Short-lived grain, prone to sprout or rot, might be broken down into flour or transformed into beer and therefore kept a little longer; we could not possibly eat the fat abundance of herring the fishermen bring back at the height of the summer from the vast silver shoals, and so we salt them in barrels for when we might need them again. The ten thousand transformations which we as a species have learned to work upon the foods we eat are almost a way of fighting the seasons, which demand that we feast for months and then starve; or perhaps they are a deal we make with them, borrowing a little here, depositing a little there, balancing the books of our year-round diet. Technological advances both in production and in storage have of course disrupted this dealing, as well as making it, for much of the world, unnecessary; it is to the credit of humanity, I think, that for pleasure and tradition we still engage in an activity we have no real need for. It would seem that as long as we have gluts of white or oily fish or green walnuts or rich milk we will be doing our best to halt their decay, and that is something to be celebrated; there are, however, other paths we can take.

As soon as we break an ingredient, the rot sets in; we can arrest this a little, but it is unavoidable. One way of dealing with this, however – in fact a way that is almost universal across the eating world – is not to arrest it, but to let it happen, and even to encourage it upon its way – to control, as it were, the manner of its dying. This is far easier than it sounds, and the barriers are rather more mental than physical. All you need, really, is to adjust what you mean by decay. When a plant or an animal dies there are both internal and external forces that begin to take hold of it. On the one hand, you have the enzymes within the digestive system, which begin to break down cell structure and nutrients; on the other, there are bacteria, moulds and yeasts of all kinds, which feed on the flesh for purposes of their own, with varying outcomes. We are taught, as cooks and really as people, too, to have a terror of decay, as proximate as it is to death. The manifold health and safety procedures, the powerful cleaning chemicals and the closely monitored temperatures of the professional kitchen or of industrial food production are all there to halt it; one hint of mould or even of yeast is enough to render a whole vat of whatever it might be apparently unfit for human consumption. Microbial life of whatever kind, in other words, is treated as an enemy to be eradicated. Some microbes of course, including some occasionally present in food, are capable of doing us a great deal of harm, but the vast majority are not; many are in fact essential for our wellbeing, living in close symbiosis with our brains and our guts, boosting our immune systems, telling us when we are hungry and what we are hungry for, affecting our moods and our tempers. We have evolved together, and for many thousands of years before our modern war on bacteria began, we were learning to live alongside them.

In a way, this coexistence is just an acceptance of the inevitable. We, the food we eat and the air we breathe are surrounded by and filled with teeming microbes beyond number, each in their way searching for food and for shelter; you can either pitch yourself headlong against them or accept their presence and what help they can give, and it is a mark only of our growing arrogance as a species that we ever thought to abandon the latter path. Our gradual return to it, luckily, has made itself felt in a number of ways, not least of which is the so-called revival of many traditional food practices, particularly those involving fermentation. This word, which covers a bewildering array of culinary preparations and which adorns an increasing number of books and recipe blogs, is really just another way of saying decay – but a tightly controlled decay, entered into in partnership with the responsible microbes. Once their ingredients are picked or chopped or crushed or dried, the fermenter or charcutier or vintner, instead of allowing any passing bacteria a foothold, creates an environment in which only one or two favoured sorts can really thrive, whether through temperature or aeration or salinity, and then lets them work. To perform any of these tasks successfully is really to accept that after a certain point your own contribution is finished, and that while you can continue to monitor and measure and adjust and taste throughout the rest of the process you are really only doing so for appearances' sake. Your work here is over, and theirs has just begun.

Another way of putting this is that these things take time – some far less than the steady but sterile work of souring and others considerably more, but in any case in much less predictable measures. To the variables of ambient temperature and of the exact condition of your ingredients, which really affect all of the recipes gathered here thus far, we are adding the totally unpredictable one of life, which can hurry along or saunter according to its own particular whims. None of the practices and recipes that follow makes use of the lab-grown bacteria you can buy to streamline the process of fermentation, nor even of the kind of natural but nurtured cultures used to make kombucha, sourdough bread or yoghurt; they rely solely on what is called wild fermentation – on the yeasts, bacteria and moulds that are everywhere around us but which vary wildly from place to place and from season to season. A kitchen full of fermenting jars, such as that of the restaurant where I used to work, will have its own little ecosystem, and we found that everything placed within it would be bubbling merrily away within a matter of days, boosted by the little lives floating everywhere around; a friend, on the other hand, found her flat in London a tomb compared to her family's house in Ukraine where she had learned to ferment and pickle, the country breeze and the abundant cellar combining to breed a fertile air.

What this means, practically speaking – and I am aware that this might sound as if I am making pre-emptive excuses – is that these recipes for fermentation are not exact; if you ever come across one that is, you can be sure it is lying to you. The usual, more or less precise timings of recipes gape and yawn out into three-to-five or seven-to-ten days, or around twelve months; what this means is not that the desired result is similarly vague, but rather that it is up to you to determine when your concoction is ready, when the bacteria or yeasts have completed their silent work to your satisfaction and when, to put it plainly, you are happy to eat the cabbage or ham or whatever the aged thing is. In the following notes and recipes I have given as much guidance as I can on this, describing what to look for in the depths of your jars to discover what exactly is happening in them, and whether it is success or disaster, but really there is no substitute for experience – and experience begins with taste. Although it is not always practical, you should as far as possible treat fermentation as you would any other part of cooking, and taste at every step of the way – from the moment you break your ingredients open, to the careful adding of salt and seasonings and the gradual souring as the microbes take control of their adopted environment – ageing and fermentation being in many regards the culmination of everything we have done so far. You cannot control everything that is happening, but you can at least pay attention to it – in fact, the less control you have, the more attention is necessary.

I said that fermentation meant rotting, and this is true as far as it goes; every application of it in the kitchen or in the cellar could, with other elements and in other circumstances, be condemned as decay. But it is also a living process, an active process, capable of rendering swift and happy change upon the most unlikely of ingredients – much, you could say, like cooking. The word itself comes from the Latin *fervere*, to boil; if you have ever fermented anything you will understand why. Most of the bacteria and yeasts we employ in the kitchen give off carbon dioxide as they feed, which forms the bubbles in Champagne and lager, the spongy holes in bread and gives the fizzy tang to kimchi. Wine, in particular, in the first few days or even hours of its afterlife, almost as soon as the juice flows from the crushed grapes, bubbles as vigorously as a pot of water on a quick fire. We know, of course, that it is not boiling – that no heat is being applied to it within or without; we know also that if we were to boil it, everything responsible for this mysterious action within it would die. The analogy stands for more than just the visual, however, as fermentation can wring a change from ingredients and leave them totally transformed as much as any combination of fire and water. As our jars, our pots, our demijohns and our amphorae bubble away in cupboards and cellars and odd little corners, we know that they cook without heat.

Sauerkraut

The German word for this recipe is one that seems somehow to have stuck, applied to a near-universal recipe. Almost every cuisine across the world and across history has adopted the products of fermentation as part of their foundational flavours, from breads and cheeses and alcohols to the more complex processes of miso and soy sauce, and more often than not this includes some kind of fermented vegetables; as I have said, it is only really the seemingly squeamish British who avoid them in favour of our more straightforwardly sour vinegar pickles, regarding any other kind with either amusement or alarm. Sour cabbage for us, then, distinct from the thickly cut pickled red cabbage of the British larder, will apparently be eternally German, despite the fact that variations of it are made in Sweden, Russia, France, Ukraine, Georgia, Turkey and Armenia, in China and Korea and Japan, and that it appears to have been known to the ancient Romans; it is not even a recent addition to the British diet. I believe the first time I heard of sauerkraut was in reading that Captain Cook would take barrels of the stuff on long voyages for its ascorbic properties. Unfortunately his crew, being as superstitious and suspicious as sailors everywhere, refused to eat this strange foreign concoction, even as the gums receded from their teeth and old scars began to gape open; eventually despairing, he labelled the barrels as 'for officers only', and soon found the men clamouring for a little of this rare delicacy.

This latter story is something I read in a children's history book and have never seen repeated since, so I cannot vouch for its accuracy; if nothing else, it has the neat and truthful ring of a very good lie.

What is certain, however, although Cook may have got the idea directly from German or Dutch sailors, is that wherever vegetables are fermented, some variation on shredded and salted cabbage is found. Some food historians would have you believe that this is due to an unbroken chain of influence that may have started with the Romans or perhaps the Mongols, who having found that cabbage, chopped up and packed in barrels with a judicious amount of salt, took on a pleasing sourness instead of rotting, carried this invention with them to the ends of their empire, whichever one that may have been. A more probable explanation, to my mind, is that like pasta, bread and alcohol, sauerkraut was a discovery waiting to happen – one that has been made again and again throughout human history. It may seem like a coincidence, perhaps, that cabbages and other brassicas so often form the basis of these ferments, but that is really just because they ferment so well. I do not know – although I would like to – the exact science behind this, but there is something in the sweetness, the bitterness and the peppery heat of cabbages of various kinds, and turnips, kohlrabi and so on, and presumably therefore in the particular combination of microbes they thereby host, which lends itself extremely well to fermentation. There is almost, in the pungent aroma of fresh cabbage, whether cooking quietly on the stove or simply cut in a heap, a decaying hint of the sauerkraut to come; it is as if the vegetable *intends* to ferment. Given this, and given also the extreme simplicity of the process, it is unsurprising that it is so universal.

Individual recipes within the wide banner of fermentation can be generally classified in two ways; the kind of microbe used, and its manner of cultivation. Alcohol, for example, is fermented with yeast, initially in the presence of oxygen, which is what makes it alcohol. That yeast, however, might come from any number of sources. Traditionally, breweries and vineyards might cultivate their own varieties of yeast, keeping from each brew a little of the spent yeast in order to maintain a certain continuity of method and flavour; now yeasts of all kinds can be isolated and grown in laboratory conditions and bought by the home or professional brewer to achieve the desired effect. Originally, of course, alcohol would be fermented with the native yeasts found on the ingredients and in the air, an occasionally unpredictable method known simply as 'wild fermentation'. Only a very small proportion of alcohol is still fermented like this, although the fashion for it is growing. Belgian lambic beers, fermented in huge open tanks, rely on the peculiar microbiome of their breweries – and perhaps of their brewers – for their sour complexity, while so-called natural or low-intervention wines use only the abundant yeasts that cover the skins and stalks of their grapes. By and large, these are considered eccentricities within the wider world of drinks, with the romantic ideas of terroir subordinated behind closed doors to the predictable rigour of science. But with vegetables, wild fermentation is still very much the norm, perhaps because a certain pungent sourness is expected.

So much for the manner of cultivation. As for the type of microbes the sauerkraut maker cultivates, the method is known broadly as lacto-fermentation, and the agents of it are lactic acid bacteria of various kinds. The first thing to clarify is that this in no way involves milk. Although they can, and do, feed on lactose, and their cousins are those responsible for kefir, for viili and for cheese, they are named as such simply because the bacterium was first observed in yoghurt, not because they are exclusive to it; they will feed also on fruit and vegetable sugars, and are what make sourdough, injera and pumpernickel sour. In other words, they are universal – they cover everything that grows, including ourselves, and although I have heard of people making sauerkraut and the like with commercially grown starter cultures, it is entirely unnecessary; the main concern of the fermenter is not in introducing the correct bacteria but rather in cultivating it and excluding the others. Fortunately this is easily done. Like everything, really, the lactobacillus feeds on sugar, which is present in everything we might care to ferment. If you simply shredded a pile of cabbage and left it to itself, lactobacilli would feed upon and colonize it, but then so would everything else, moulds and yeasts as well as any other bacteria which might happen to be around, which is where the salt comes in. Salt is inimical to microbial life – and indeed to all life in sufficient quantities; bury yourself in salt and you would find that you had not long to live. The many and various permutations of undersea life, meanwhile, are largely structured around protection from their briny world. The use of salt as a preservative is predicated on this as well as its dehydrating properties.

Lactobacilli, however, are tough. In their various forms they can tolerate a great deal more acidity than the majority of bacteria – they can breed unchecked without oxygen, and they can handle salt; not in vast quantities, but certainly in higher concentrations than mould and yeast and their cousins who might do us harm. The phrase 'good bacteria' (not to mention its associate phrases of 'helpful' or 'useful' bacteria) is not one I have much time for. The splitting of the natural world into the parts we can exploit and the parts we cannot, or even worse into some kind of moral hierarchy, is a particular disease of humanity I feel it is best not to encourage, but it is difficult to avoid the thought, when you consider the various properties of the lactobacillus and the cornucopia it helps to create, that it was put upon this Earth in some way to aid us. Another way to put this, I suppose, would be that it has evolved alongside us for a million years and continues to do so, adapting every hour to its new environment. Just a small amount of salt, in any case, works in sauerkraut to keep out unwanted life and allow our lactobacilli to flourish, feeding on whatever we give them and producing in return lactic acid, which in turn breaks down the sauerkraut further, protects it even more closely against other microbes, and gives the whole a pleasing sourness, gentler than the puckering of acetic or citric acids, but with a particular living musk of its own. Lastly, all of this happens in a more or less airless environment, thanks to the combination initially of salt and force, whether that force be gently massaging or pounding with a mallet designed for the purpose, which together draw out the juices from your cabbage, keeping it safely submerged in its crock or jar while the bacteria feed and sourness prevails.

In the simple fermentation of vegetables – which could be cabbage of the white or red or pointed spring varieties or equally, in their seasons, turnip, daikon or black or large red radish, knobbly celeriac, beetroot, the slim bulbs of wild or spring onions, good sweet carrots or bitter green stalks – we can see all these methods come together, an edible history in brief of cooking without benefit of heat; fitting really, when you consider that the process has been with us almost since we were human, that some of the earliest evidence we have of culinary activity lies in fermentation pits, as far apart as Sweden and old Mesopotamia. Of course, fermentation of one kind or another would happen by itself were humanity to be entirely removed from the face and depths of the Earth, as it does today in fizzy windfall fruit and piles of browning leaves as the heat of the summer draws to an end; all we are doing is guiding it, nudging it this way and that towards our chosen destination.

You can use almost any spices for a sauerkraut – caraway, fennel seeds, juniper berries, whole peppercorns, dried chilli and nigella seeds all work well – or none at all. I like the way mustard seeds accentuate the mustard tendencies of cabbage, which makes for a good all-purpose sauerkraut. You can also vary the cabbage. Red is excellent, turning at the point of souring a rich and bleeding violet, while the flat Turkish and the pointed varieties both work very well, too. I would steer clear only of savoy, which lacks the required juices in its crinkled leaves.

1 large white cabbage
coarse sea salt
1 tbsp mustard seeds

Peel off the outer leaves of the cabbage, cut it into quarters and remove the core. Shred the quarters finely with a sharp knife or on a mandoline, then weigh the prepared cabbage and transfer to a large bowl.

Measure 2 per cent of the cabbage's weight in salt – for example, if you have 1kg of cabbage, you will need 20g of salt – then add this, with the mustard seeds, to the cabbage.

Mix the salt through then massage it into the cabbage with your hands, rubbing and crunching the cabbage until it starts to release its juices, in a similar but more forceful manner to the kebab-shop onions. You are really trying to break the fibres of the cabbage; when you can wring out a handful like a wet cloth, it's ready. Pack into glass, ceramic or plastic jars or pots, making sure there are no air pockets and that the liquid completely covers the cabbage, weighing it down if necessary with a small jar or well-washed stone, then cover tightly. Ferment at room temperature for around five days, tasting after the third.

For all the mystery around fermentation, you can consider your sauerkraut ready when you think it is ready; when it has reached the point of sourness and crunch that you yourself like. If you want it to stop fermenting, you can put it in the fridge; the cool will slow the process almost to a standstill. You may, on the other hand, wish to see what happens if you leave it to its own devices; just remember, each time you remove some kraut from the jar, to pack what remains back beneath the surface of the liquid, to keep it safe from the air.

Fizzy Tomatoes

Although in these notes, and in every guide I have written or lesson
I have taught on the subject, it is sauerkraut that comes first (as
I believe it to have been in culinary history), it is not where my own
interest in fermentation really began. My first attempt at sauerkraut,
in fact, was a total disaster; the recipe I followed was unclear as to the
proper method, and at that point I knew nothing of the requirements
of the bacteria we associate it with. I tried, in short, to ferment my
cabbage not only without properly salting and massaging it, but in
an open and airy container. Quite dry and open to the elements, it
was quickly covered first in a pungent yeast and then in mould, and
the smell, as you may imagine, was quite overwhelming. This put me
off the idea of sauerkraut for a little while, as I concentrated on other
kinds of pickles. At around the same time I made a kind of kimchi,
although of a fairly tame sort. Fermentation had not really taken hold
in Britain, even to the limited extent it has now, and the idea of simply
leaving food at room temperature for days on end, especially when it
contained not just *nam pla*, which as a bottled sauce is accepted in the
national mindset as shelf-stable, but also dried fish rehydrating in the
juices of the kimchi (in this case not the shrimp the recipe demanded
but some desiccated anchovies brought back from Turkey), was
anathema to the popular cookbook. The recipe I used asked you first
to salt your vegetables overnight and then, with seasonings added, to
keep the lot in the fridge, where whatever fermentation might happen
would be slow and mild. The resulting kimchi, although tasty, had
little of the pungent funk I had hoped for; fermentation had again, it
seemed, let me down.

It was not until some time later, working at the restaurant in Suffolk, that I came back to the process, faced as we frequently were with seasonal gluts of various vegetables and fruits. My parents, as I have mentioned, grow vegetables, and I was familiar with the idea of these yearly abundances – that over the course of the summer you might have to eat rather a lot of courgettes. For the first time, however, I felt this abundance as an urgency, the seasons almost something to fight against if we were to make the most of them. I remember keenly the sense, on the first day of September, that what life we had now would have to last us through to the spring – although given that we also had access to wholesale vegetable suppliers this was perhaps a little dramatic. In any case, during the course of my time there I became gradually more interested in various crafts of the kitchen, learning a little butchery, baking sourdough and teaching myself to make charcuterie, and it was perhaps inevitable that I came back also to fermenting vegetables, not at first with sauerkraut but rather the sour salt-pickles of further east. The particular spark for this re-emergence into fermentation was the vast profusion of tomatoes I mentioned before, some soft and dripping, to be eaten like a peach over the sink, others almost crunchy. Throughout the height of the summer we made salads every day, dressed only in their own sweet juices – to the point, if I am honest, that I was sick of the ripe and ruddy sight of them. At this point, summer drawing to an end, the remaining plants gifted us with something like twenty kilograms of green fruit, a last-ditch attempt to breed destined never fully to ripen. I made ketchup with them, I pickled them in vinegar, I salted them like umeboshi, and eventually I turned to a recipe that had caught my eye in Olia Hercules' book *Mamushka* for little fermented tomatoes, a speciality it would seem of Ukraine. Unlike many recipes in English for tomatoes, which demand some impossible dream of Mediterranean ripeness, this asked specifically for underripe and perhaps disappointing examples; having now made it many times, I think it is the best use for much of the fruit commercially available here, although that is perhaps not saying a great deal. It is still better, in any case, to begin with good ingredients, underripe though they may be.

Crucially, the recipe seemed also extremely simple, with fermentation neither presented as some harnessing of bizarre forces nor glossed over entirely, but rather as a method of the home kitchen as homely and familiar as baking a cake, the attention paid to the process in much of the UK and the anxiety it seems to cause many – including at one time myself – nowhere to be found. Essentially, the mystery was removed; where many guides to the subject – including perhaps my own preceding section – seem to seek to induct you into some sort of secretive guild of fermenters, insisting that you understand fully the esoteric movements of bacteria before you lay hands on a cabbage, these recipes are given simply as ones which work, to be followed as you follow any other, and so I did. That I later self-inducted myself into this guild, learning as much as I could about the process and about the possible errors and dangers, is neither here nor there. As far as I am able, I like to understand everything I do in the kitchen, with heat or without, and if fermentation has particularly caught my imagination and inspired me to learn more than in other cases then it is only a matter of degree; I believe it to be in some sense the duty of anyone who considers themselves a craftsperson to learn, at least to some degree, the hidden dimensions of their chosen profession. In any case, the point is that my first really successful attempt at fermentation was done really in a spirit of confident ignorance, following blindly in the footsteps of an expert – and there was nothing wrong with that. If you wish, you can ferment – or indeed follow any recipe, within this or any other book – without troubling yourself particularly about the process you are helping to enact, and often you will get better results by doing so. It often seems to me that it is only when we start to doubt ourselves that things go wrong.

Once your beginner's luck is gone, though, and doubt creeps in, as it inevitably will, you will find that you need to know your subject a little more thoroughly in order to work out the problems that begin to occur. This is especially true in fermentation. I am sure I have spent more time in my life explaining what can go wrong in making sauerkraut or pickle than in discussing the pleasures of what can go right; the endless permutations of disaster seem always to fascinate us. Although my early attempts at sauerkraut were all destined to fail, and although the largest single quantity of mould I have ever witnessed was removed from the top of an otherwise perfect crock of red sauerkraut, once I got the hang of the process I found it to work reliably and consistently, even with small adjustments when, for example, using completely different vegetables or when fermented in the dog days of the year as the jars beaded with sweat. Conversely, despite my initial successes I have found fizzy tomatoes, along with other salt pickles, to be much more temperamental. This may be, I suppose, because much more depends upon the fruit itself. Even taking into consideration differing varieties, ages and seasons, a cabbage is a cabbage, and whatever individuality it once possessed is to an extent eradicated in the course of shredding, salting and pounding. A fermented tomato, on the other hand, like its cousin the gherkin (in methodology if not in genes), is left whole, suspended not in its own juices but in a manufactured brine. The finished pickle is much more reflective of the raw state of the fruit than sauerkraut is of the cabbage – the condition of the fruit, it should be said, being also much more varied in tomatoes and cucumbers than in brassicas.

Quite apart from the fruit, of course, is the matter of the brine. Sauerkraut is all one thing, and there is only so much that can go wrong with it; with brined pickles, the problems are, in a sense, doubled. You have first to worry about the condition of your vegetables or fruit and then about the strength of the brine, and once fermentation has begun and sourness taken hold, you have in turn to pay attention to your softening pickles and to their salty bath, susceptible as it is to any number of maladies. It is important with all cooking that you trust in the method you are using, and especially so with fermentation, where you must place a great deal of faith in the workings of time and salt – and I certainly have no desire to add to the fear of decay and the unknown that seems to put so many people off the practice. It is equally important, however, to recognize that things can and do go wrong, and that while most of the time they are salvageable, occasionally they simply are not. Again, though, this is the case with all cooking, and I have certainly lost fewer ferments over the years than I have burnt cakes, curdled sauces, overcooked pasta and ruined eggs; if fermentation requires a greater investment of time than any of these processes then at least that time is not your own. In any case, total disaster can usually be averted if you simply pay attention to your ferment, and I would always advise you to keep your jars or crocks somewhere that is visible to you as you go about your daily life.

The most obvious failure of fermentation is for fermentation simply not to happen at all. You may find that after a few days your jars are showing none of the visible signs I mentioned before – no bubbles and no cloudiness creeping through the brine. You may begin to worry, and think that you have done something wrong. If you have followed the practice carefully, then it is most probable that fermentation is simply taking its time. Perhaps it is a little cold in your kitchen, or in your town, or perhaps the vegetables you used were especially well-washed and therefore lacking the full spectrum of bacteria; perhaps you just used a little too much salt. Generally, the solution to this is patience. Colder weather could mean the early stages take a week or more to get going, and heavy salting can double that time; it would take a really strong concentration to totally inhibit fermentation, to the point of inedibility, so I'll assume you haven't done that. If you have, however, or if you haven't but you would like everything to move a little faster, you can simply dilute your ferment, pouring off some of the brine and topping it up with fresh water.

If it is very hot, on the other hand, you might find that your ferments are far too active, and that they soften into a mush before they are as sour as you'd like. The best cure for this is prevention – in summer, I tend to use a little more salt than usual, and to put my jars somewhere as cool as possible. If your ferments have gone very soft there isn't much you can do about it beyond using them for cooking instead of eating raw; not an entirely bad thing. Contrary to what many seem to think, some fizziness is good in your ferments; these tomatoes in particular, the fermentation enclosed in their taut skins, offer a distinct sharpness on the tongue. That said, if you notice a ferment fizzing spectacularly within a few hours of making it then try to move it somewhere a little colder, even the fridge. Fermentation is almost imperceptibly slow under refrigeration but it does carry on, especially if it was very active to start off with, and it is better to end up with a jar of something nice in two months' time than a jar of fizzy mush in two days.

Even with the salt levels exactly right and with fermentation proceeding at a desirably stately pace you may encounter a few problems, most caused by invaders, and it is these that seem to worry people the most. Friends and acquaintances are constantly sending me pictures of the tops of their crocks and jars with the caption 'Is this mould?' or 'Should I throw it away?' The answer to both of these questions is generally 'no'. If you make a few sauerkrauts and brined pickles it is extremely likely that you will at some point encounter a sort of white, powdery substance on their exposed surface, especially if the vegetable is poking out of the brine. This is not mould but yeast, and it is one of the main reasons for using salt when we begin, which inhibits its growth considerably. The body of a mature ferment, teeming with lactic acid bacteria, is safe from invasion, but the surface is vulnerable to the airborne microbes; luckily yeast is largely harmless. You can simply push your kraut beneath the surface and perhaps weigh it down a little better, and scrape the yeast off if it really bothers you. I tend to just stir it in. At worst, you may get a variety called kahm yeast, which forms a much thicker layer of soft, folded whiteness across the surface of your brine; I particularly get this in sweeter ferments, and find that it is quite contagious once it gets into one of your jars. Kahm yeast is still harmless, but it does give off a pungently yeasty smell that can infuse into your ferment, so scrape it off thoroughly and have a taste of the vegetables beneath. If you're happy eating them, then they're fine.

Mould, it should be said, is a slightly more fraught subject; quite apart from the taste of it – reminiscent in the back of the mind of something damp and deadly, of caves and the underside of woodlouse-ridden logs – there are many kinds that will do you some harm if eaten or even if breathed in too deeply. Here, though, we can still let our senses guide us; white mould, like that which covers soft cheeses and good salami, can be scraped off with impunity, while anything blue, black or red should be treated with care; throw away the contents and begin again. I have no wish, however, to dwell on failure. This recipe, as I said, has served me well – perhaps better than any across the years – and all it really needs is for you to begin well. Start with the right tomatoes – maybe green and unripe but in any case firm and crunchy while still well-flavoured – and seal them properly within their jar, and you should have little cause for alarm; they ferment quickly – you can watch them do it, and count the days before you can enjoy their sour sweetness, their delicate and brutal effervescence.

1kg small green or underripe tomatoes
a few lovage or celery leaves
25g sea salt
2 cloves of garlic, lightly crushed
1 tsp black peppercorns
2 bay leaves

If the tomatoes are of a cherryish size then they can happily stay whole; if they are larger than a golf ball then cut a deep cross into the top of each one, leaving the quarters joined at the bottom. Pack the tomatoes into a jar and top with the lovage or celery leaves.

Add the salt, garlic, peppercorns and bay leaves to a pan with a litre of water. Bring just to the boil, stirring to dissolve the salt, then leave to cool completely. Pour over the tomatoes, top with a piece of scrunched up baking paper to weigh them down, and seal the jar.

Let the tomatoes ferment at room temperature for three to five days, at which point the brine should be turning cloudy and the fruit losing their intensity of colour. Taste one of them; it should be pleasantly sour with a faint fizziness on the tongue. If not, leave to ferment for a day or two longer.

Once you are happy with the fermentation you can keep them in the fridge, where they will last, happily, for ages.

(A Version of) Sardella Calabrese

Controlled decay when it comes to products of the vegetable kingdom is one thing; that of the sea is quite another. Of all the fear of rot that seems to beset our modern culinary selves, disconnected as we are from wildness and danger and almost from death, the fear of fish seems the greatest. In Britain, in fact, the creatures seem to unnerve us even when fresh; there can be few countries in the world with such a rich diversity of available seafood and yet so little inclination to eat it. On the beach at Holkham in North Norfolk, in common I'm sure with beaches elsewhere across our shores, the appearance of a perfect expanse of silver sand gives way on closer inspection to a mass of razor-clam shells, enough that to dig down or to run barefoot across it is to slice yourself to ribbons. Such wild abundance, and yet the shellfish are a rare sight on menus and on the fish stalls of markets, let alone on tables at home. The razor clam, it's true, has a somewhat alien look to it, lolling like a stalked eyeball out of its long black home, but even when it comes to ordinary round fish, with fins and skeletons, we tend to traditionally confine ourselves to a narrow range, not coincidentally reflecting that of the fish and chip shop. We don't know, it seems, what to do with the others; they might taste of mud or of the slimy depths, they might have organs or appendages that even in death may poison us, they might too readily go bad.

We have already discussed the somewhat misguided reverence for freshness when it comes to fish, and seen what salt and a little time can do for it and for our cooking; even for devotees of aged, raw and cured fish, however, fermenting the things might seem a step too far. Casual discussions I have had on the subject tend to centre around words such as 'stench' and 'botulism'. This is ridiculous, really, when you consider that fermented fish was once one of the most common forms of seasoning in Europe, as indispensable as salt, and that it is still so today in much of South East Asia; perhaps many people here simply do not think of it as such. I no longer remember when I first read about garum and *liquamen*, the ubiquitous fish sauces of the Romans, but I recall – I'm sure in common with many people – that my initial reaction to them was disgust. Any passing description of these condiments and cooking sauces, before (or often instead of) mentioning their possible flavour and their culinary applications, seems required to mention that they were made not just from fermented fish but from fermented fish *guts*, and furthermore that their production was so noisome it had to take place away from major metropolitan areas for fear of widespread sickness and disgust; it rarely seems to acknowledge the fact that, as far as we can make out, liquamen in particular was essentially identical to *nam pla*, part of ten thousand preparations which range from the subtle to the sledgehammer – as sauces should.

It is interesting that the apparent taboo around this very common preparation of mainly small pelagic fish – oily anchovies and their cousins – should centre on the use of their offal, our traditional disgust at the non-muscular flesh of animals mingling with our suspicion of the sea and our fear of decay to produce something like a perfect storm of horror. It is the guts that really get you; even the hardened consumer of liver, kidneys and blood might balk at intestines in any other context than the skins of sausages, which have been thoroughly cleaned and salted, and in any case these days are often synthetic. When eating the true andouillette or the *stigghiola* of Palermo (sheep intestines wrapped around a spring onion and barbecued to a somewhat uneven crispness), it is hard to forget that what you are eating once contained shit. With smaller creatures we do seem to gloss over this somewhat; although land snails are generally left to purge themselves of excrement before we cook and eat them, molluscs of the sea usually are not, and sprats and whitebait, once fried, are eaten entire. In the case of fish sauce, anyway, the guts are in fact essential; without them there would only be rot.

Mere wild bacteria, as effective as they are in other situations, are not strong enough to work on the mercurial flesh of fish as they do on cabbages, tomatoes or even the flesh of land animals. If you salted and mixed a kilogram of cleaned, fresh anchovy fillets and left it to its own devices then the inevitable result, although slowed by the salt, would be a heap of stinking decay – the kind of thing many people perhaps imagine when they think of an ancient garum factory, set on some sun-beaten shore that even the seagulls avoid. That fish sauce does not smell like this but rather rounded, deep and savoury, is thanks not to bacteria but to digestive enzymes within the guts, which break down the protein of the fish into amino acids, the physical embodiment of umami. Some people, in fact, would argue that this process, involving as it does not separate microbial entities but a part of the once-living animal, should not be considered fermentation at all, but rather a distinct and as-yet unnamed category. This is a largely semantic issue that I do not intend to get involved with; what is certain is that transformation of a profound sort is taking place, brought about in this case not so much for physical edibility as for the demands of flavour.

When discussing the modern use of the anchovy in Italian cooking there is a temptation to forge with it some link to the imperial past – to see it as the descendant somehow of garum, although really in flavour it is quite unlike it. For all their depth, fish sauces taste clean and somehow clear, matching well with the brightness of citrus and chilli and vinegar, whereas salted anchovy fillets have, I think, something murky to them – a meaty opacity which infuses anything cooked in their company; this is strange, as the production methods of the two are really very similar. Although anchovies destined for tins or jars or vacuum-packs will generally have their heads removed, they too are left otherwise whole and are layered with salt to age, fermenting with their guts in place until the flesh turns the same sort of rich, reddish brown as a good fish sauce. This again takes some months to achieve, and again is not something I would particularly advise you to do at home; it is mostly a fully industrialized process, requiring a temperature somewhere between cellar and ambient difficult to achieve without dedicated equipment – and even if it did not, fresh anchovies are quite hard to come by in Britain. Consigning any you do find to an uncertain process of which the best possible outcome is a poor imitation of a product you can readily buy seems to me wasteful.

You can do the same thing, it should be said, to most proteins; the same principle is at work, for example, in the various misos and soy sauces of Japan, China and elsewhere. Made chiefly of pulses and grains, of course, these lack the natural digestive aids of fish, but in these processes they are added in the form of one or another kind of *koji*. Grains, usually of rice or barley, are inoculated with a particular breed of mould, which as it feeds and develops produces the same sort of enzymes as in garum, breaking down the proteins present in soya beans and wheat into their constituent parts, again in pursuit of a rich and deep flavour. By any method, to be clear, this takes a long time. I have made fish sauces on a number of occasions, some inoculated with fish guts and some with barley koji, and they have all taken at least six months to come to anything approaching deliciousness. All of them, I think, could have done with a great deal longer, either in their initial fermentation or in a second ageing in bottle or barrel, in order to reach their full potential. They certainly needed longer than the patience of my co-workers would allow for these odd buckets and jars of murky liquid. Even if not rotting as such, the smell fish sauce gives off is still distinctly bodily, that of iron and seaweed and strange fluids; it is not a project I would necessarily recommend for the home cook.

Cooking with it is, however – and especially investigating the ways it is used in cuisines we may not think of as based around fermentation as such. Take, for example, the somewhat nebulous cuisine of Italy, insofar as it exists as an entity distinct both from the thousand local cuisines of which it is comprised and from the imagined Mediterranean diet as a whole. In the mind's eye, as with sushi, Italian cuisine is something that seems to revolve around the fresh and the abundant, around market stalls in the heat of the summer piled high and wide with tomatoes, aubergines, green beans, courgettes and their spiralling leaves, peaches, plums, cherries and great bunches of herbs, or alternatively fish and seafood glinting under shade in a hundred shades of silver, striped and scaled and with tentacles coiled around little handwritten signs. It is something, in other words, which seems based on produce, where other less fortunate countries must rely on process. This, of course, falls apart almost as soon as you begin to think about it. Alongside this wealth of fresh life, which in any case can be difficult to find either on restaurant menus or on tables at home, comes of course the trinity of wine, bread and olives, typical not just of Italy but across the Mediterranean, give or take national and religious customs – all three not just processed, but in fact fermented in their various ways. Although the country in the main has no great love for lacto-fermentation, other kinds are in fact ubiquitous.

Italian cooking, of course, is not homogenous, and it possesses stranger corners and permutations than many outside of the country would give it credit for (as well as many within it); products not just of the Italian soil and of generations of nonnas, but of the waves of immigrants and occupiers who for thousands of years have brought their recipes with them. This seems especially visible, for some reason, in the cuisine of the south, the offerings of which thrum in the heat, with flamboyant rococo pastries and spices and condiments of all kinds, far beyond the somewhat austere simplicity we might imagine for the *cucina povera*. Although Sicilian cuisine fascinates me, both in its baroque excess and in its mountainous clarity, I find the cooking of Calabria particularly intriguing, dominated as it is by a heat of chilli far beyond the tolerance of most of the country, apparently a legacy of the Spanish. Its most famous product outside of the region is probably 'nduja, etymologically linked to the French andouillette and andouille but in form most similar to the Balearic *sobrassada*, a spreadable cured sausage with a high proportion of fat; the Calabrian iteration is, in addition, made up of one-third chilli of various sorts, both dried and pulped, and is capable of being extremely spicy. Although chilli is poorly understood in comparison to those of salt and acid, it – or rather its active principle, capsaicin – possesses curing properties of its own; it is certainly antimicrobial, and plays a major role in the complex balance of, for example, kimchi, in which some ingredients suppress and others feed its fermenting bacteria. It is unsurprising that where chilli is popular, it forms an important part of traditional methods of fermentation and preservation.

Much less known than 'nduja outside of Calabria, and to me more interesting, is *sardella calabrese*, a sort of spread or condiment made from the tiny squirming fish known as *neonata*, fermented whole in salt and chilli. Alongside its Spanish heat, it seems also to speak of ancient ferments – of vats of fish lining old southern shores. It works, I assume, on the same principle as salted anchovies and garum, with enzymes within the digestive systems of the fish breaking down their flesh into an umami-rich result. It is delicious; I have only had it brought back for me from Calabria, and have never seen it for sale elsewhere. As much as I would love to make it, it isn't really possible in Britain. I have never been quite clear on the legality of fishing and selling neonata within Italy, although you certainly see them in markets everywhere, but they are not something you can buy here. You could perhaps try to make something similar with sprats, but the same problems of time and smell apply as with the manufacture of garum; it is simply quite an antisocial activity. The idea of fermenting fish in chilli intrigued me enough, however, to develop this version, which is really not in any way like the original, either in method or final form, and risks bringing upon me the wrath of the cooks of Calabria. Recipes travel, however, a wise cook once told me, and sometimes they change along the way.

This recipe has a number of stages and may seem at first glance a little complicated; none of the steps is difficult, however, and the fermented pepper paste is a very useful condiment to have around, for stirring into a bowl of chickpeas or a salad.

For the fermented pepper paste
8 large red peppers, halved and deseeded
coarse salt
2 garlic cloves, crushed

Roughly chop the peppers and then weigh the flesh. Measure 2 per cent of the weight of the peppers in salt and mix together. Pile the peppers into a colander and leave overnight at room temperature.

The next day, blitz the salted pepper with the garlic as finely as you can – a blender is ideal. Pour into a jar, leaving a good 10cm of headroom – this is an extremely active ferment – and seal. Leave to ferment for three days, then store in the fridge.

For the (version of) sardella calabrese

50g sea salt

25g caster sugar

500g sardine fillets

2 large red peppers

100g fermented red pepper paste (see above)

30g red pepper flakes

1 tsp chilli flakes

1 tsp fennel seeds

Mix together the salt and the sugar and layer this with the sardine fillets in a non-reactive container, finishing with a layer of sugar and salt and making sure they are all thoroughly coated in the curing mix. Cover with cling film and refrigerate for twenty-four hours.

Rinse and dry the sardines then lay on kitchen paper in the fridge to dry out further for another hour or two, or overnight at the most. At the end of this they ideally should feel slightly tacky to the touch; this is the perfect texture for taking on their chilli cure.

Meanwhile, prepare the marinade. Roast the peppers over an open flame, placing them directly on the hob and turning until the skin is blackened all over; if you don't have a gas hob then you can grill them or roast them in a very hot oven, where they should take around twenty minutes. In any case, once the peppers are thoroughly blackened, place them in a bowl and cover with cling film. Leave until they are cool enough to handle, during which time they will steam and soften further, then peel and deseed them. You should find that the skins come off easily. Place the roasted flesh in a food processor with the fermented red pepper paste and the spices and blitz to a loose salsa.

Mix the resulting sauce with the sardine fillets and pack tightly into a clean jar or a ceramic or plastic container. They should be completely coated in the pepper mixture but it will not necessarily cover them like the liquid in a pickle. Seal the container and place in the fridge for at least five days; you are looking for the fermenting acidity to cook the fillets in the same fashion as pickled herring, although they will remain somewhat firmer. Once cured, they will last in the fridge for at least two weeks, developing as they rest.

You can eat the fillets as they are, perhaps on toast with chopped parsley; I like them chopped up and tossed through chubby pasta shapes with their marinade and some crushed walnuts.

Cured Sausage

For all my talk of fermented fish, obscure combinations of pickles and organs, soured milk and brutalized octopus, I think if forced at gunpoint to choose my favourite food, it could well be a sausage. It is a constant that is comforting in its bewildering variety, from the deep-fried and eerily smooth tubes of supermarket café breakfasts to the raw and hand-chopped sausage of Bra in Piedmont; almost everywhere across the world that meat is eaten, it is stuffed into skins to be cured or cooked. The pork and fig leaves described earlier might represent one extreme of this, almost totally unlike most Western examples but still in some sense recognisably a sausage, being highly seasoned, wrapped, tubular. Within the European tradition, the accepted narrative is that sausage making derives from the Romans, who spread the practice to the limits of their empire along with alliums, celery, brassicas, lagomorphs, stone fruit and many herbs (it is difficult to imagine what exactly the ancient peoples of Britain, particularly – isolated as they were – ate before the arrival of the Celts and then the Romans). According to this theory, every iteration of – to put it broadly – meat stuffed into offal, from *botifarra* to bratwurst to haggis, forms part of one family tree that perhaps stems ultimately from one ancient cook, maybe Roman or Etruscan or Greek, who first decided to mince part of their pig and place it inside another part. As neat as such tales are, I have always found them somewhat unsatisfying, whether rooted in historical fact as the present narrative or as clearly fantastical as the tale of the Chinese swineherd; how easy it is to credit the lone genius, the flash of inspiration or the civilizing invader with what in reality happens again and again in different places and times, the work of many hands across slow generations. Any invention that is both useful and pleasing, culinary or otherwise, is bound to be repeated across thousands of years, or so it seems to me – and sausages are certainly both.

A sausage is useful firstly because it is economical. It is easy to deride hoof-and-eyeball hot dogs as an unwholesome product of our industrial food system, but really it is the point of a sausage to contain hooves and eyeballs; you can put prime cuts into one if you like, but both the mincing, which in some cases pounds and reduces the meat almost to a pâte, and the usually heavy seasoning allow tougher and less palatable parts to be easily incorporated. In the past, I have made sausages from the parts of a sheep that essentially I couldn't use for anything else – meat scraped off the bone, solid fat and skin – which were good; I have also made them from the boiled lungs of a couple of pigs, which were excellent. A sausage skin covers any number of sins, and in fact often turns them into delicacies. Think of a haggis, for example, which takes most of the internal organs of a sheep, mixes them with a handful of oats and stuffs them into another organ, the result being not subsistence fare but a once-yearly treat; sausage making is useful because it is transformative, in this and in other ways. We often make a distinction between fresh and cured sausages, between *saucisse* and *saucisson sec*, or between *salsiccia* and *salame*, as if they were completely different things, although really we can say that all sausage is cured to an extent. The seasoning, firstly, which might be applied directly to minced meat, or alternatively to cubed meat which is left overnight to lose moisture before mincing, has an inevitable curing effect, the inexorable work of salt upon flesh helped also by the subsequent sausage skin, strong but breathable. Although in Sicily I have had sausage stuffed to order for me by a small-town butcher, any handmade sausage you buy in the UK will probably have been hung at least overnight in a large and airy refrigerator, allowing the seasoning to take proper hold and the skin to dry a little into something that will brown nicely in the oven or on the grill. Some butchers will use harsher saltpetre in their fresh sausages, but even with sea salt alone it is this brief curing process, I think, as much as the rich fat and the distinct mixtures of herbs and spices, which differentiate various local recipes and which makes sausages so particularly satisfying.

Thus far we might find sausages to be broadly similar to other forms of cured meat and fish, from the quickly salted loins and cod presented earlier in this book to fully aged charcuterie, and to an extent it is, in practice; we weigh, we salt, we check for moisture loss and textural change. Sausages differ, however, in one key regard, and that is directly related to their grinding – the breaking. The interior of a muscle, such as a leg for ham or a collar for coppa, is sterile – there is nothing in it that can harm. We protect the exterior, draw out moisture from the centre, and charcuterie results. This sterility is lost the minute you cut into it and bacteria flood in. We cannot stop this from happening, and so when the meat for a sausage is cut, we need instead to direct these bacteria, to encourage one sort and discourage the others to produce something that is both safe and hopefully good to eat; when you age a sausage, in other words, you are not just curing it, but fermenting it. Salami is firstly broken, then salted, then soured, then aged; it is the culmination of everything we have done so far.

Although you might imagine meat to be particularly troublesome to ferment, it is not especially so, particularly in comparison to fish. After the slow action of enzyme upon protein that comes directly from the animal or from mysterious cultivated moulds, we are back to familiar territory – to essentially the same process that governs sauerkraut and other fermented vegetables and fruits, that of simple lacto-fermentation. Of course other factors are at work within and without a curing sausage, most obviously the bloom that may or may not cover its skin, but that is all, really, at the start of the process, which concerns us.

To my mind, then, the difference between, say, a fine Lancashire sausage and the mould-covered, misshapen puddings you see at food markets everywhere alongside the paella and the olives is chiefly one of degree; any sausage, or at least any sausage with enough salt, has within it the capacity to become salami. Another Sicilian butcher of my acquaintance – a proud if faintly sinister Palermitano – did, in the course of a lengthy demonstration of his craft, make what he considered a fundamental distinction between salame, which contains curing salts and is generally made by a specialist, and *salsiccia stagionata*, or 'seasoned sausage', which is cured with salt alone for a shorter period of time, being the size of what we might consider a regular sausage, rather than the hefty widths of most salami; I did not, to be fair, fully understand what he was saying, but in any case I don't think the difference is quite as clear-cut as he made out. Fully fledged salami by whatever spelling can be made without curing salts, and any kind can be cured really for as long as you like, with the main factor to consider being what sort of thing you want to eat at the end of the process – something soft and almost spreadable or something dry to be chipped off in little shavings and chewed like jerky on a long march.

The question of how you achieve this, however, is especially fraught, particularly in the USA, where the absurd under-regulation of livestock farming has inevitably resulted in an equally absurd over-regulation of certain aspects of food production; the question, essentially, is of how much intervention you choose to have – whether you play it safe with nitrates and added bacterial cultures or whether you let nature take its course. On the one side, we might say that salami has been made for thousands of years without such additives, that such caution is simply a product of our modern fears; on the other, we could point out firstly that nitrates have been used in the making of salami for a very long time, whether as trace elements in unrefined salt or deliberately processed and added, and secondly that our modern fears have, in fact, resulted in longer lives and the near-eradication of certain diseases. Personally, I have never used so-called starter cultures, while the question of curing salts or nitrates is one I struggle with. Their purpose, essentially, beyond the use of regular salt, is the eradication of botulism, an unpleasant and potentially lethal disease that attacks the nervous system and shares its etymology with *boudin* and pudding, the name coming from the Latin for sausage, *botulus*. The botulism bacterium breeds without air and can tolerate quite a large amount of salt – and it takes very high temperatures to kill it. As well as sausages, it is a lover of poor canning, as the crew of Franklin's lost expedition found out to their cost. Given all this, you might think that the answer to the nitrate dilemma is clear, but of course nothing is. Nitrates firstly bring with them a somewhat unpleasant flavour, a slight synthetic tingling which once you have noticed is hard to ignore, and secondly they carry health risks of their own, being linked to cancer even in the tiny amounts used. Luckily, however, there are other weapons that can be used against botulism. In common with most microbes, it has a low tolerance of acidity, and this is where the fermentation comes in.

Without wishing to become too technical, all that is required to make your curing sausages safe from botulism is a moderately acidic environment with a pH less than 4.6 (recall those strips of paper, the transforming colour bleeding across them – the lower the pH, the higher the acidity). To be clear, 4.6 is not especially sour. Strong vinegar measures at around 2.5 and fermented pickles in the region of 3.5, while most wine sits somewhere between 3 and 4. Almost all fruit, for example, is sour enough to keep itself safe from harm if otherwise properly treated and canned. Introducing lacto-bacterial cultures to your salami, along with sugar for them to feed on, is certainly one way of ensuring that a safe level of acidity will be quickly reached, but it is by no means the only one. Adding a decent proportion of red wine, in my experience, keeps the acidity low enough while you wait for natural fermentation to begin, and within a good margin of error. The point, in any case, is that while I am familiar with the numbers above, have spent hours with a pH reader, have endlessly debated with myself the use or not of nitrates and starters, it is only because it has been my job to do so; selling fermented sausages to unsuspecting members of the public is very different to doing so in your own home, where so long as you follow certain rules and proportions you need nothing more specialized than an airy place for them to hang as the summer heat begins to fall.

Try to get your meat from a decent butcher, and tell them what you are doing with it; ideally they will mince it for you as you watch. You will need a sausage stuffer to make this at home – you can get a hand-cranked one quite cheaply. Alternatively, if you are especially friendly with your butcher they may make up the sausages for you if given the mix.

> *hog casings*
> *1kg pork mince*
> *300g pork fat, minced*
> *45g fine sea salt*
> *1 tbsp black peppercorns, toasted and ground*
> *1 tsp fennel seeds, toasted and ground*
> *4 cloves of garlic, minced*
> *250ml red wine*

Soak the hog casings in cold water for a couple of hours.

In a large bowl, mix together the meat, fat and salt thoroughly, then add the spices, garlic and wine. Continue mixing by hand until you have a fairly homogenous mixture.

Pack the mix into your sausage stuffer and load the soaked skins onto the nozzle. Crank the stuffer until the mix reaches the end of the nozzle, then tie off the end of the sausage skin tightly like a balloon. Fill the casing slowly, working the filling down with your hand so there are no pockets of air. You can either twist the salami off into small sausages as you go or leave it in one length. Once you have used all the filling, cut and tie off the skin and tie each end together to form a loop.

Hang your sausage (or sausages) in the kitchen or airing cupboard or otherwise somewhere warm overnight to start the fermentation, then transfer to a cooler and airier spot, perhaps by an upstairs window or in a shed. They do not like to be too dry; if after a week you can feel that the skin is hardening while the meat within is still quite soft, then keep a tray of water underneath the hanging sausage to increase the humidity.

Individual sausages should take a couple of weeks to cure, while the larger salami should take around a month; check it every few days by giving it a squeeze. Once it feels fairly firm to the touch, it is good to eat, but you may wish to leave it longer for a drier salami. Transfer the sausage to the fridge when you are happy with it, but bring up to room temperature to serve, to enjoy the rich fats and the fermented tang.

An Impractical Lesson in Ham

We are moving away somewhat from the bounty of summer. The heaps of bursting red tomatoes and even the later desperate greens, the thousand flashing herring and the dripping peach trees all sit in the past; the rolling hills of Kent or Sicily or Ukraine have long since turned from their spring brightness to a darker green and finally an exhausted gold, the land is worn out, as everyone is, the heat has nothing left to give and everything is aged and drying. There is still work to be done, though, as impossible as it may seem. Those fermented sausages, really, are not traditionally the product of summer, or at least only of its very tail end; in places where the summer is not too warm for such methods it tends to be too wet. For this, and I'm sure for many other reasons – some practical, others perhaps verging on the magical – pigs are killed in the autumn, then butchered and salted and fermented and hung, with some of the resulting products to be eaten across Christmas and the winter and some to wait for next summer, with a fresh load of its bounty; transformations continue to occur, even if the lowering skies might start to demand more in the way of actual cooking.

In a sense, I suppose, even the pig itself is an example of this transformation – of cooking without heat – turning as it does in the course of its fattening life from food that is otherwise discarded or inedible to us – the swill of kitchen scraps which used to be the staple diet of the family hog, the rich acorns of the woods – into something entirely other, in this case the tissue of a living creature, which in turn will become other things to eat. If this seems a little stark then I can only apologise; it is the way things are. Everywhere across the world, in the wide blue skies and the depths of the seas, food is turned into food and again into food, dies and changes and is food again. This is as true in the microbiome of a jar of sauerkraut as it is in the macrobiome that most of us live in, and it is important, therefore, to remember that a lot more goes into our food than what we ourselves add to it during the processes that are under our control of breaking, curing or cooking. We worry about eating swordfish or tuna not just because they have been overfished into a dwindling remnant of their former glories, but because in the course of their comparatively long lives they ingest more of the poisons and pollutants we have leaked into their world than younger fish can, the toxins staying in their body and becoming part of the food we make of them, whether in steaks or in jars or in tins. I imagine there is a lot more we should worry about eating, in this increasingly filthy world. I forage for soft fruit in the side streets of cities, and I wonder.

More positively, we might think about what goes into the plants, and especially the animals, we eat to give them flavour, nutrition and succulence, and about the way we turn the landscape we live in into the food we eat. Outside the very literal fact that plants take life from the soil, much of this, it is true, is impossibly romantic. I remember distinctly being told in an early kitchen job that the meat of game, I think specifically wild boar, was so special because you could taste within it the wild herbs it had fed on in Scotland or Dartmoor or the Ardennes or wherever the creature was shot, which struck me at the time, sceptical teenager that I was, as being particularly unlikely. What a lot of game tastes of, in comparison to conventionally farmed meats, is the remnants of the adrenaline flooding its tired body mingled with its subsequent decay – rather medieval ideas about hanging game still being somewhat fashionable. In any case, it seems improbable that flavours which don't even survive long cooking times should be discernible through the course of digestion and transformation into muscle. What does seem to be the case, however, is that flavours consumed as fat are laid down as fat and that their oils are transferred from plant to animal more or less intact, especially through the simpler stomachs of omnivores; this is why, according to a recipe I have for their ham, you would be advised not to eat bear during the salmon season. More generally speaking, this is why we do not tend to eat carnivorous mammals and birds, although we are much less picky when it comes to the sea.

The pig, in fact, is one of the few really omnivorous creatures of the land that we have made a part of our diet, which is one reason why their meat is considered unclean in two of the Abrahamic religions – even though, practically speaking, the meat component of their feed will generally amount to little more than a few beetles and worms grubbed up from the ground. It depends, I suppose, on what goes into their swill – although since the catastrophe of BSE it has been illegal to feed to pigs the food waste that once made them so practical to keep. In any case, it is not animal fats but those from other sources that we wish to feed to pigs, especially when we are going to eat the results cured but raw, in preparations considered the pride of pig keeping wherever they are made. The most prized charcuterie of Spain, for example, comes not just from the black-footed pigs of the region but specifically from those that have fed upon acorns in the final stages of their life, the foraged feed lending its rich nuttiness to the abundant fat which crowns the hams, dripping down them into little stalactites as they hang from warm rafters; this feasting on acorns was once widespread across Europe in the semi-wild herds of pigs that predated industrial farming. The delicate flavour of the prosciutto of Parma, on the other hand, supposedly comes in part from the whey the pigs are fed upon, a by-product of the region's famous cheese. Whey, again, used to be a staple of the farmhouse pig's diet; 'There's nowt wasted where a pig's kept,' as my grandmother used to say occasionally – I think more apropos of my own appetite than in regards to the animal as such.

What this means from the perspective of the home, or even the professional cook, is that any recipe – for cured ham in particular but also for any preparation of ingredients that is not then cooked – wherein the transformation made is subtler than that of heat and smoke, can only go so far; your consideration has to begin much earlier, while what you intend to eat is still alive. Of course this is true to an extent of all forms of cooking, and countless recipe books will tell you of the importance of shopping, of finding ingredients at their best and their most seasonal, which have been farmed well and handled well on their way to the buyer – but nowhere is this so starkly apparent as in the case of an air-dried ham, where the produce in question is not just raw, but concentrated, with whatever qualities the pig possessed magnified in the mouth of the eater. This is why this lesson in ham making must really be considered at best impractical; even a book such as this, which deals with recipes in months rather than hours, cannot encompass the life of an animal – even the comparatively short lives we generally give to those we eat. Should you wish to take up pig keeping, you will have to find another book on the subject – or you may wish instead to find a farmer or a butcher who seems to be treating their stock well, and ask them questions about it. Come to think of it, you may think it better, while you are at it, to find someone already making good ham from such well-kept animals, and to buy it off them; there is a certain obsession for the house-made among chefs that I have myself often been guilty of – a sort of bunker-mentality insistence on doing everything yourself, when we could instead be fostering a community of specialists, each pursuing their own kind of excellence. Still, if you find yourself in possession of a leg or two of pork, then the lesson is here if you need it. The reason, finally, why this lesson should be considered impractical is that I have never in fact made a ham by dry-curing the entire leg of a pig; as a teacher, here I am a fraud. This is, however, only because such a thing has not yet come my way. As I write this in the dying heat of summer there are two pigs fattening for me, a spotty sow I call Borlotta and the black boar Salsiccio, and in autumn they will die. Ham, coppa, cured sausages, blood pudding and brawn are all to come, but too late to write about here; for this I am sorry. I have, however, made charcuterie of many other kinds – some from pigs, but mostly from sheep and from goats, as it was a farmer of these ungulates who approached me at the time I wished to learn about fermenting and air-drying meat. You cook with what you have in front of you, and try not to wish it were anything else. In any case, these much smaller animals turned out to be ideal to learn on, taking much less time than the plump muscles of a full-grown pig to cure; I am told that their fat, being somewhat inclined towards rancidity, is considered a challenge to age successfully, but I have never found it much of a problem. As I mentioned earlier, my first attempt at curing of any kind was with the whole bone-in leg of one of these sheep, and it turned out fine – better than fine, in fact. The process is in any case identical for different animals, the differences only being those of weight and time, and so these loose instructions hold true for whatever you might want to cure, be it pig or goat or even bear.

A slightly more practical recipe to begin with, which should fit in your fridge for the first stage; this is not unlike the method used earlier for carne salada, but its bath in wine is shorter and it is afterwards dry-aged. In addition to the ingredients, you will need butcher's string and access to an airy place such as a drafty room or a shed.

1 whole pork collar
coarse sea salt
750ml red wine
2 tbsp black peppercorns
2 tbsp fennel seeds

First, weigh the pork and make a note of it (you will need this later, as well as for the quantity of salt). Measure out 3 per cent of its weight in salt and rub this all over the pork, then place the pork in a deep, non-reactive container and pour over the wine. It doesn't matter if the meat isn't entirely covered – you'll just have to turn it every day or so to make sure it is evenly marinated. Cover and refrigerate the pork for a week.

Once the pork is marinated, wash and dry it thoroughly before tying it into a tight roll with butcher's string. You can either do this in separate loops or in the continuous knot butchers use; the latter is difficult to describe, so I would stick to the former unless you can watch it being done.

Coarsely grind the spices and mix them together, then rub this all over the pork. Hang it in an airy place, perhaps by an upstairs window, with something under it to catch any drips; it is ready to eat when it has lost 35 per cent of its original weight. Once you have cut into it, store it wrapped in the fridge.

I am assuming that your fridge will not fit an entire leg – even of a goat – so this recipe uses what might seem like a frightening amount of salt. It does need somewhere fairly cool for its first stages, so this might be something to keep for the beginning of colder weather.

1 leg of pork, goat or sheep, bone in
coarse sea salt
a few bunches of rosemary branches
2 tbsp wine vinegar

First, weigh the leg and make a note of it. Measure out 10 per cent of its weight in salt and rub this all over the meat. Make a layer of half the rosemary in a non-reactive container, place the meat on top of this and cover with any loose salt and the rest of the rosemary. Weigh the whole thing down with a few tins or something similar and leave to cure for two days per kilogram of meat. While, thanks to the salt, it does not need to be refrigerated, the meat should not be too warm at this stage. Well covered in a shed or a large windowsill would be ideal.

When the time is up, wash and dry the meat thoroughly then rinse with a couple of tablespoons of vinegar. Wrap it in muslin or in one leg of a clean pair of tights and hang it somewhere reasonably airy. As with the pork collar, you are looking for around 35 per cent weight loss, but you can monitor it at first simply by squeezing the meat; you will feel its gradual change from raw meat into cured. This is a long process; even a goat leg will take a couple of months.

When you slice into it, leave a flap of the exterior meat and fat to keep the cut surface covered. You can first enjoy the sliced ham as it is, then begin to cook with the offcuts as you would pancetta or bacon, and then finally, once the rest is stripped clean, make a good, rich stock with the aged bones.

CONCLUSION

I introduced this somewhat disparate collection of notes with the observation that summer is fleeting; that even the dragging dog days come, in time, to an end. In fact, by the close of the season I am often glad to see the back of it, which is exactly as it should be; to put it another way, I am usually looking forward to what autumn has in store. A large part of this, however, is what we have borrowed from the summer, the abundance of heat giving us not just immediate pleasure but future sustenance. We should make the most of our summers, of course, but as we have seen, wringing the utmost from the season will often mean looking towards the future and laying down defences against it. We say that we should make hay while the sun shines as if it means we should live for the moment, when really the saying warns us to marshal our resources against the coming cold. Part of the task of the conscientious cook has always been to ensure that when Persephone prepares to go back beneath the cold ground, she goes along with jars and crocks and barrels of pickles, ferments, chutneys, pastes, jams, cheeses, salted and soured meats and all the other edible memories of warmth that are made possible by the ripening heat.

The summer passes, and once it does it has passed forever; everything we have picked and broken and cooked within it will never be done so again, and nothing can go back to the way it was. That does not mean, however, that it is over. If we cannot fix what is broken, we can do something different with the debris – something better, maybe, but at least something new; we can use all the various methods of transformation to subtly alter our ingredients again and again. All seasons are fleeting, of course, and all of them give us abundance of a kind – something to enjoy today and something to bring forward into the next, through salting or drying or whatever means. Nowhere, however, is the ingenuity to do so felt and needed as much as in the lethargic heat of the summer, with the knowledge of the winter to come, when we have to work not just against time and decay but against our own exhausted sweat. It is a time to step away from the kitchen, and indeed out of the house altogether; a time for holidays, yes, for eating raw shellfish in close proximity to the sea, for evenings passed in an endless procession of little snacks and freezing beers, but it is also a time for the hard work of harvesting and processing, salting and hanging and barrelling, in fields and in workshops and on ships.

The recipes I have collected here tread a perhaps uneasy path between these two sides of the summer – some meant to be enjoyed in a moment, others designed to last through months or even years of careful storage; but what they have in common, I think, is greater than what divides them. Together they provide, if not an exhaustive compendium, then at least a guide to all the ways we can alter our food without coal, gas or induction. I said at the beginning that I do not intend this book to be a raw food manifesto, in part to distance these ancient processes – as old or older than humanity – from any notion of faddishness or fashionable modern diets; I would like to add that this is also because I have no wish to discourage people from cooking. I am a cook, I like to cook, and furthermore few of the recipes in this book really create standalone dishes in the conventional sense. They are intended to be used as components within a larger meal, notes of rawness or salt or sourness to complement or contrast with other elements that may be grilled or roasted or braised. The macerated onions, for example, make sense only alongside charred and sticky meat, while nothing complements a crisp pickle so much as soothing boiled beef; these are additions to your cooking repertoire, not replacements for it.

Looking beyond the recipes, which really are intended only as demonstrations of a wider principle, the techniques and processes described are all ones that can be incorporated more generally into your cooking, whatever the season and whatever your ingredients; they are something else we can borrow from summer to see us through the rest of the year, alongside that cornucopia of produce, those gluts upon gluts which fill kitchens and jars. There is more potential in a piece of beef than steak and chips, more to a plump white onion than the beginning of a stew. Not everything you cook might need pounding like an octopus or ripping along its grain like a plump mozzarella, but it all needs to be broken in some way – sliced or ground or smashed; thinking about the different ways you could do this and the different dishes that might result is one way of thinking about cooking. Or take salting: cure meat for long enough and you can eat it sliced and raw, but you can also salt it briefly before cooking for a firmer texture and a half-cured depth. Fermentation, finally, is used across the globe both as a substitute for cooking and as a complement to it. While much of its popularity in Britain focuses on the health benefits of fermented vegetables and drinks as raw products, its traditional uses are for preservation and for flavour; miso, soy, fish sauce, aged cheese, sour cream and vinegar are all fermented products which are not necessarily an end in themselves, but rather one stage in the continuous process of transformation that turns the raw components into a meal. These are skills that simply offer a different way of looking at your ingredients – more closely perhaps than you otherwise might, to think for a while about what might be done to them both at and away from the stove.

These notes are, I hope, also satisfying in their own right, providing as they do a pleasure in cooking and preparing food at a time of the year when there might otherwise be little pleasure to be had in the sweating humidity of the kitchen – demonstrating that the shining of the sun does not necessarily mean we have to reach immediately for the charcoal and the grill but can instead take a gentler, slower approach that stretches perhaps over days or months; the steady enjoyment of tinkering with something as it ages, the sudden delight as a once-unpromising jar at the back of the cupboard comes out completely changed. More than anything they serve as a reminder, if only to myself in the restaurant kitchen, that not everything is within your command – that although you can choose the ingredients you put in and the circumstances of their cooking, sometimes you have to step back and allow, as it were, nature to take its course. To put it another way, when you are cooking you can decide upon your end result and control the process every step of the way – or, alternatively, you can set something in motion and see where it ends. While it is perhaps not entirely suited to the professional demands of consistency and customer satisfaction, it is this latter course I find myself increasingly drawn to. Who wants their cooking to be as open and closed as a solved equation, always reliable, always the same, when it could instead offer itself up like a flower – like the beginning of a koan that is yet to be asked...

what cooks

without heat?

INDEX

ACKNOWLEDGMENTS

Thank you to

ADRIANA
FABRIZIA
LIBORIA
RACHEL
and
TERESA

in whose houses I wrote this

PRAISE FOR THOM EAGLE'S
FIRST, CATCH

Winner of the Fortnum & Mason
Debut Food Book Award 2019.

First, Catch was also nominated for the 2018 André
Simon Food & Drink Book of the Year, and included
in BBC Radio 4 Food Programme, *Financial Times* and
The Times' 'Best Food Books of 2018'.

'A wonderful taste of fresh air ... *First, Catch* is almost
revolutionary ... His words are delicious, musical heaven'.
William Sitwell

'Thom Eagle's writing is pure joy – effortless and
unaffected. He is easily one of my favourite writers,
and this book deserves to become a classic'.
Olia Hercules